The Ultimate Musical Theater College Audition Guide

D1496172

The Ultimate Musical Theater College Audition Guide

ADVICE FROM THE PEOPLE WHO MAKE
THE DECISIONS

AMY ROGERS SCHWARTZREICH

OXFORD
UNIVERSITY PRESS

OXFORD
UNIVERSITY PRESS

Oxford University Press is a department of the University of Oxford. It furthers
the University's objective of excellence in research, scholarship, and education
by publishing worldwide. Oxford is a registered trade mark of Oxford University
Press in the UK and certain other countries.

Published in the United States of America by Oxford University Press
198 Madison Avenue, New York, NY 10016, United States of America.

© Oxford University Press 2019

All rights reserved. No part of this publication may be reproduced, stored in
a retrieval system, or transmitted, in any form or by any means, without the
prior permission in writing of Oxford University Press, or as expressly permitted
by law, by license, or under terms agreed with the appropriate reproduction
rights organization. Inquiries concerning reproduction outside the scope of the
above should be sent to the Rights Department, Oxford University Press, at the
address above.

You must not circulate this work in any other form
and you must impose this same condition on any acquirer.

Library of Congress Cataloging-in-Publication Data
Names: Schwartzreich, Amy Rogers.
Title: The ultimate musical theater college audition guide :
advice from the people who make the decisions / Amy Rogers Schwartzreich.
Description: New York, NY : Oxford University Press, [2019] |
Includes bibliographical references and index.
Identifiers: LCCN 2018030328| ISBN 9780190925055 (pbk. : alk. paper) |
ISBN 9780190925048 (hardcover : alk. paper)
Subjects: LCSH: Musicals—Auditions. | Acting—Auditions.
Classification: LCC MT956 .S4 2019 | DDC 792.602/8—dc23
LC record available at https://lccn.loc.gov/2018030328

This book is dedicated to all my students: past, present, and future.

CONTENTS

"Let's Start at the Very Beginning"

H ello there, my name is Amy Rogers Schwartzreich, and I am the director and founder of the BFA Musical Theater program at Pace University in New York City. I am passionate about training the next generation of Musical Theater artists and have had the great privilege to watch and nurture hundreds of students as they follow their dreams of being a professional actor.

If you are a high school student, or the teacher/family member of one (known as the "team" from here on), who is looking to embark on the journey of studying Musical Theater at the university level, then there is a strong chance you are feeling overwhelmed about how to even begin this confusing, rigorous, and competitive process.

The good news is, I am here to help! I started the Musical Theater program at Pace sixteen years ago, and I have since sat in on over 15,000 hours of college auditions. Combine that with my role as an acting teacher who specializes in song interpretation, repertoire, and audition technique, as well as my experience as a professional director, and you will see I am in the unique place to guide you through the college audition process from beginning to end.

This book will talk right to you, the auditioning student, but is useful to everyone helping you through this experience. The tone is direct, up-front, and perhaps even harsh at times, but know that it comes from a place of respect, compassion, and a deep understanding of this process. I know what you are going through. I have watched countless students take on this journey with wide-ranging results, from extremely successful to choosing another route altogether, and because of that, I really know what it takes. Hopefully, hearing from the people who make the final decision about your admittance into a program will give you the most insight to help you through the process, with the least amount of stress and anxiety as possible.

This book will focus primarily on the BFA Musical Theater audition process, but we will touch on other options as well. Much of the advice given here can be applicable to other kinds of audition-based programs or auditions in general. The information here is a consolidation of *best practices*. Because of that, what you will read is through the lens of not only myself, but also faculty and professionals from around the country who audition and recruit, teach and direct, and run programs at the university level. There are as many opinions as there are programs (as you will see from the input from my colleagues), and while we share many similar points of view, an acceptance decision can ultimately come down to things that are beyond the control of the auditioning student. My hope is that you can maximize what you have control over and let go of what you don't.

That being said, all art is subjective and in many instances unquantifiable, so what will work for one program may not work for another, even if the book suggests so. You could follow every suggestion written here and still not get into a program—and that, my dear reader, is the reality of this industry you wish to join.

Every program that you audition for will vary slightly in its requirements. Program reputations will change and new programs are developed every year. If you are reading this book, you are most likely passionate about Musical Theater; you know you want to study it in college and then make it your career. If that is the case, you are embarking on a lifetime of learning and it begins now. Stay organized, make lots of lists, and research (research, research) to find the best program for you. You don't need to have all the answers now—the book will help!

I advise talented high school students who want to pursue a career as an actor to undertake postsecondary education. College is a bridge from student to adult, from dependent to independent, from learner to thinker, and from just being someone who is talented to someone who has competetive skill. A specialized degree will give you the foundation as a person and artist to navigate this complex and emotional career.

The real truth is that you do not need a BFA in Musical Theater to be a professional actor. In fact, there are numerous successful, working actors who never even went to college. What you *do* need in order to be a working professional in this highly competitive field are expert skills, a mighty talent, and deep dedication, and I believe that college programs can help you find, fine-tune, and focus these attributes. As with most things, there is no one formula for success, but the life and technical skills you get from pursuing a degree are essential and can create the foundation for a lifelong career.

I will leave you with one piece of advice before we begin: no matter what, you need to BE YOURSELF and do what is right FOR YOU. All the advice in the world will be meaningless if you are going against your gut. Trust yourself and listen to your instincts because, ultimately, you are your best guide.

Now, let's begin!

ACKNOWLEDGMENTS

I t is with great admiration, respect, and gratitude that I thank all those who contributed book chapters: Stephanie Layton, Sean McKnight, Grant Kretchik, and Wayne Petro.

I am extremely grateful to Jen Littlefield, my book editor. Without her, this book would not be possible.

My intent was for it to be a "best practice guide," and that could only be done by gathering points of view from a variety of colleagues, including the following:

Robert Meffe, San Diego State University
Gary Kline, Carnegie Mellon University
Mark Madama and Jason Debord, University of Michigan
Barbara MacKenzie-Wood, Carnegie Mellon University
John Simpkins, Penn State University
Catherine Weidner, Ithaca College
Bob Cline, Pace University, Casting Director
Michelle Chassé, Boston Conservatory at Berklee
Kaitlin Hopkins, Texas State University
Victoria Bussert, Baldwin Wallace University
Roger Grodsky, Cincinnati Conservatory of Music
Joe Deer, Wright State University
Tracey Moore, The Hartt School, University of Hartford
Robin Lewis, Rider University
Hank Stratton and Danny Gurwin, University of Arizona
Matt Edwards, Shenandoah Conservatory

Brian DeMaris, Arizona State University

Andrew Byrne, Voice Teacher

Christian Flaherty, photoshop and photo editor

Mary Anna Dennard, Founder of I Got In, http://collegeauditioncoach. com

Chelsea Diehl, Founder of My College Audition, www. mycollegeaudition.com

Halley Shelfer, ArtsBridge Consulting, http://artsbridge.com

Susan Woodell-Mascall, http://www.collegeauditionpro.com

Ellen Lettrich, Musical Theater College Auditions (MTCA), http:// mtcollegeauditions.com

Very special thanks goes to these special people:

Gayla and Brian Rogers—parents and role models

Lauren and Foster—my loves

Introduction

MY INTENTION FOR THIS BOOK is that it serves as a best practices guide. It is full of information and advice from not only me, but also my colleagues who teach at a variety of universities around the country. You will see many opinions that are similar and some that are completely contradictory; that is the nature of this process and the theater business as a whole. Because of that, you have to decide for yourself what information feels right and authentic to you, and know that if you try to please everyone, you run the risk of losing yourself in the process.

There is not one way to move through the college audition process. In fact, the more you think about this as rigid or formulaic, the harder it may be. Art is subjective, and there is truly no way to know what every school is looking for at any moment. What you can do is figure out what you have control over and what you don't, let go of the things you cannot control, and focus on the rest. If you are able to do that, this journey may teach you more about yourself than you ever imagined. And it might actually be, wait for it . . . fun!

I realize this process is big and often all-encompassing, but it can also be very manageable and almost easy if you focus first on *preparation*. One thing I stress throughout the book is to keep everything organized. I cannot say this enough to you. Keeping all the different requirements, dates, and program details in an easy-to-find location, whether it's a notebook, a bulletin board, or a folder on your desktop, is key (could there be an app for this?). It will give you something to turn to whenever you have a question or need to double-check that you are on track with material choices or deadlines. Organizing the chaos of applying to many programs can help you manage the parts of this process that are within your control, when so many other factors are unknown.

Before reading, I recommend that you arm yourself with a good set of tools to help you through this long journey:

- Keep a highlighter or pen handy so you can identify things in the book you want to easily find later.
- Figure out how you like to process information. Do you like to read everything first and then go back to the individual chapters and advice as needed? Or do you want to put the skills into practice as you read them? Neither way is better, but knowing how you work before you start can make the process move smoothly and help you not become overwhelmed.
- Have your notebook or computer out, and be ready to write down any action steps or lists you want to start.
- Create different sections or folders with easy-to-identify titles, such as "School Options," "Song Choices," "Program Requirements," and so on, to help keep all the information together.
- Within each section or folder, brainstorm ideas, write down your feelings, and make comparison and pro/con lists. Auditioning is a long process and many things will change as you go, but having a record of programs that caught your eye, or how you felt when you sang one of your possible audition pieces, will help you remember all the little details that can easily be lost along the way.
- If you're feeling stuck at a particular part of the process, the chapter takeaways are a concise recap of the main points of each chapter, and they can guide you through the steps needed to complete the task.
- When in doubt, return to your lists and create new ones if necessary.

Now that you are ready to dive in, remember that I am/we are all rooting for you to be the best version of YOU throughout the audition process. If these tips, tricks, and pieces of advice can help you achieve that, wonderful! I wrote this book to arm you with as much information as possible in the hopes that demystifying the "unknowns" of the process would help you relax and be present in the moment. But if these practices are not what's best for you, then figure out what WILL make you shine and go forth with confidence.

1 | "Learn Your Lessons Well"

APPLYING TO PROGRAMS

There are a variety of excellent schools where you can begin your Acting/Music Theater education. Do your research. Look at each school's curriculum. Look at what their recent graduates are doing and where they are working. Be clear of your goals and ask yourself honestly which school feels like the best fit for you. Then, spread your audition "net" wide. Have a variety of schools you are applying to. Make sure you have both "reach" schools and a few that you know you can get in to.

—Barbara MacKenzie-Wood, Raymond W. Smith Professor of Acting,
Carnegie Mellon University, School of Drama

Where to Start?

Regardless of the major, the college application process can be complicated, time-consuming, confusing, and expensive. Add to that the research, preparation, and travel for program auditions, and you can see this is no easy task. This journey you are about to go on can start as early as your sophomore year of high school and then last through the spring of your senior year. If you are late to the game, don't worry; there are many different pathways through this process, so keep reading. Think of it as the first investments you are making in your future career. The skills you hone and utilize, and the habits you create during this hectic time, will only help you better handle the rigors of academic life and, eventually, the often less-structured "real world."

I am not trying to scare you, only arm you with as much information as possible so you can tackle this process head-on. So let's get started!

Your Team

If possible, you should not go through this alone. Your junior and senior years are hard enough without all of this on your plate. Between schoolwork and keeping your grades up, all of your extracurricular activities and training, there is not much time or brain space left over to be fully in charge of the audition process. Build a team of helpful individuals you trust so you can set yourself up for success. This does not mean that you are asking other people to do your work for you: you are simply asking for support. You should know everything that is happening, including dates, deadlines, and requirements, but your team can be incredibly valuable to you in many ways.

> **Tip 1:** Your team is one of your most valuable assets to this process. These people are parents, relatives, teachers, mentors, and so forth, who can help you navigate the application process. Everyone has a different team and each member of the team will have different skills they can contribute to the process. You can't be expected to do this on your own, so build your team with people whom you trust and who have your best interests at heart.

Steps to Finding the Right Program for You

Your very first step—which ideally should happen toward the end of your sophomore year or beginning of your junior year—is to start exploring which kinds of programs interest you. There are countless ways to study Musical Theater after high school, and finding the right kind of program in the right kind of school for you is key. Many external factors come into play as well, such as cost, location, degree type, and program focus. It seems daunting at first, but just like anything, once you research all the options available, you will feel much more in control of the decision. Every step of the way you need to remind yourself that you love this art and you want nothing more than to do it for the rest of your life!

> *Do not get tied up in the idea that you have to go to a specific school because everyone says that school is great or because it appears on a top ten list. You have to find the right fit for you. You need to be at a school where you feel a connection to the faculty, where you feel like you fit with the students, and where you think you can get the best education for your investment.*
>
> —Matt Edwards, Associate Professor and Coordinator of Musical
> Theatre Voice, Shenandoah University

- Degree Type

I suggest first deciding what degree type is right for you. Essentially your options are a BFA, a BA, a BMus, or a certificate-based program. I will define what these are in just a minute, but this decision will help you focus your preparations on the correct audition requirements and narrow the whole application process into manageable components. Once you have done that, your job will be a lot easier. If you are unsure of your goals, you can apply to multiple program types, but know that each type of program will require a different kind of audition and audition process.

- Location

Do you want to be in a big city or small college town? Do you want to be a drive away from your home or does distance not matter? Do you want to be close to a professional theater/cultural scene and possibly start making connections outside of school? Does the area have a political aspect that makes you uncomfortable? Do you feel safe in the area? What amenities are close to the school—only a Walmart, lots of restaurant options, wildlife and nature? Being comfortable with your surroundings can be a big factor in how you like your school and program.

- The Program's Website

Look at the program requirements, the class offerings, and the department production photos. Read about the school—what is their mission statement? How do they talk about diversity and inclusion? Who are the professors and what are their teaching philosophies? Where did they study? Are you looking for a faculty of working professionals or does that not matter to you? Are they current? Is their work relevant? How does the school market themselves online and professionally, and do you feel a connection to this kind of promotion?

- Double Major, Minor, or Study Abroad?

It is important to remember that each program of study is different and not all will give you flexibility within your studies. Do you want to have a double major? Does the program let you? Do you want to travel? Does the program let you? Is there a semester abroad or the option to study abroad in the summer? This is where considering a conservatory-style BFA as compared to a liberal arts–based BA will matter.

- Social Media

Many programs will have a strong online presence. Watch videos of their recent senior showcases if they are posted. Do you like what you see? Is there diversity in the program? Do you like how they are singing? Does their acting seem authentic, grounded, and powerful? Do you like how the graduates are dressed and presenting themselves? Could you see yourself up there? Asking yourself these questions will truly help you choose the right fit. Take care to not let these videos, or a lack of them, be your only resource in this decision, as not all schools will promote their programs this way. A school may produce remarkable performers, but you might not be able to see them for any number of reasons.

- Curriculum

Does the program have a focus (classical acting techniques, an option of on-camera work, strong vocal technique, etc.) and does that excite you? Does the program of study work in a progression that makes sense to you? How many university core or academic classes are required? Every program is different, so brainstorm what matters to you, lay out a path that connects to you, and find a good match to your ideal path. Do Musical Theater majors take classes with acting majors? If so, why? And if not, why? How many private voice lessons do you get in your eight semesters? Can you work with a vocal coach in addition to a voice teacher? Are dance classes required and are they leveled in a way that match your skills?

- School Opportunities

Does the program let freshmen audition for department productions? In the fall? In the spring? Is that important to you? How many productions does the program do each year? Do you like their current or past seasons of shows? Can Musical Theater majors audition for the straight plays? What are the student-run theater opportunities on campus? Can you apply for internships? Professional mentorships? Teaching opportunities? Is there crossover into production work or just performance opportunities?

- Campus Type

Are Greek life and football teams important to you? Do you want a big university with lots of majors and extracurricular activities outside of theatrical production work? Look at the class size: is it typically in an eight-person studio or a 100-person lecture hall? Look at student life, the dorms, on-campus dining. Talk to students; talk to alumni. You won't be in the Musical Theater department exclusively, so make sure you pick an environment that will help you thrive in all ways.

- Using the Summer to Sort It Out

Most schools will have an on-campus summer program for high school juniors, where you can meet some of the faculty and work in the program's facilities. This can be a good gauge of the school, the program, and the surrounding area. Just be aware that many of the faculty members do not work during the summer and may not be there for you to meet. It also won't be an accurate representation of the student body talentwise, as the summer program may not be as competitive as the undergraduate auditions. And, most importantly, admittance into a summer intensive *does not* guarantee you a spot in the program.

- *College Confidential/Online Forums*

This website is mostly used by parents and students during the application process with specific groups for Musical Theater information. Note that while these sites can answer many questions, it can be very gossipy and not have firsthand information. In some cases, it might not even be the truth. Universities don't typically post on *College Confidential*, so make sure you are getting the facts before you take what you read as truth.

- Cost

Have a real conversation about what is possible for you and your family. Find out what scholarships, financial aid, and work-study jobs are available. Do they have talent-based and academic scholarships? Federal or program-related grants? Are you allowed to work outside of school while attending? If so, are there places near or on campus where you can work (or would like to work)? Does the student body tend to be a working group, or by and large are they mostly students who do not hold down outside jobs? I say this here and will say it again, but many programs don't have talent-based scholarships anymore. The majority of aid, grants, and scholarships now seem to come from the university primarily as opposed to the actual program.

- Academic Rigor

If you are looking for a university program that will provide advanced academics, then your college list should reflect that. There are some programs that you will find where the major is top notch, but the academic ranking is not high enough for your standards. Of course, the same goes for the reverse—you will find institutions in which the quality of the academics is extraordinary, but the major is not quite there yet. Some schools will have an honors college or honors program that you can apply to or join to help give you more advanced academic work.

Degree Options

> **Tip 2:** So much of this information is now at your fingertips and can be easily sorted through to get all the facts. Not every school or program will be right for you, no matter what their ranking or reputation (or perceived reputation) is, or how many Broadway performers they have graduated. Don't forget that reputations fluctuate, long-standing programs change, and new programs are developed all the time. It is your job to find out which options are out there and then discern which of these is the right fit for you. I cannot stress this idea enough. Don't rest your decision solely on the advice of others because they will not be in the program, you will.

Each school structures their programs differently. While a degree can have the same name (BFA, BMus, BA, etc.) the curriculum and structure and amount of credits can vary from school to school. While this may be confusing, there are some ways that these programs can be categorized.

Bachelor of Fine Arts (BFA)

By earning this degree, you'll take part in the most rigorous and immersive specialized training for Musical Theater performance. Many BFA programs are exclusive and highly regarded in the theater world. There is typically a great deal of competition to get into them, and even sometimes to stay enrolled. BFA programs are often taught in or through a *conservatory* or in a conservatory-style setting, where the focus is more on performance training and experience as compared to a liberal arts education. Students are not expected to take as many general education classes in addition to their major requirements. In a liberal arts program, the aim is a well-rounded academic education as opposed to a very specialized and focused one in the conservatory style of the BFA. Often this means that there is very little room within the BFA requirements to study abroad, double major, or "explore other options" in different departments. Some programs will build travel into their study, but it is safe to not expect that for most.

A BFA will almost always come with an agent showcase in New York (and sometimes Los Angeles) at the end of your senior year, multiple productions, and intensive and in-depth training with the ultimate focus of preparing the student to be a professional actor.

Most, if not all, BFA programs are audition-based only. These programs are extremely difficult to get into because the volume of candidates far outweighs the number of "slots" that are offered. For example, in 2018, the Musical Theater program at Pace Performing Arts had 1,700 applicants completing their prescreen video submissions. The pool was narrowed to 700 live auditions, and from there we took a class of twenty-eight. That is less than 2 percent of the initial applicants. This number will be consistent among the competitive programs. Also, for almost every institution, you must be admitted both academically and through the department performance audition to be accepted into a BFA program.

Bachelor of Music (BMus)

This degree is typically offered through a school of music, rather than a school of theater or drama. The curriculum will have been designed with music training as its centerpiece, but if the focus of the degree is "BMus in Musical Theater," then there are classes in dance and acting as well. Most of these programs will graduate excellent artists who can cross over into opera as well as Musical Theater. The audition for a BMus may also be different than those for BFA or BA programs. In addition to Musical Theater repertoire and a monologue, you will typically audition with a classical/opera selection and be asked to sing in a different language. Often there will be a music theory component. Some extraordinary Musical Theater professionals have earned this degree, and it is a wonderful option if you are inclined to have music as the central focus.

A Bachelor's of Music in Musical Theater is a competitive performance-focused degree that offers a strong foundation in music. Though these degrees tend to live in music departments rather than theater departments, many programs strive for comprehensive training in acting, dance, and theatre arts. With a strong foundation in voice, musicianship, and varied ensemble experiences, a Bachelor's of Music in Musical Theater can be a great place for students who are interested in expanding their training in classical music and opera. With the lines between musical theatre, opera, and other musical art forms constantly becoming less defined, many of these programs have a proven track record of training complete singer-actors who are skilled in a wide range of repertoire, which can be highly marketable in the 21st Century professional arena.

Brian DeMaris, Artistic Director, Music Theatre
and Opera, Arizona State University

Bachelor of Arts (BA)

This degree typically does not require an audition to get into the program. It is a liberal arts degree that is broad and flexible, and you often have the ability to pursue a double major, a minor, or to study abroad. While there are some very rigorous BA programs that produce highly skilled and deeply talented singing actors who are working professionally, this is typically not the goal of a BA program. These programs rarely have a final agent showcase for their seniors, as a showcase is not a BA student's goal in the first place. This type of degree is for students who want to be well-rounded thinkers and learners, for those who would feel trapped in a singular, hyper-focused program. Their varied experiences of study and travel can benefit professional performers in tremendous ways, and you can absolutely have an incredible career with a BA degree.

Certificate Programs

Programs like the American Musical and Dramatic Academy (AMDA) or New York Film Academy are examples of Musical Theater certificate programs in New York City. A vocational education aims to provide technical skills that apply to a specific job, in this case, Musical Theater performance. Some certificate programs are linked to a university, meaning you can go to them for your training and complete your academic classes through their affiliated university if you wish. However, you can also simply apply directly to these programs and train in a nonacademic setting. They are efficient and often take between twelve months and two years to gain a certificate of completion (this would take longer if you are pursuing a degree from the collaborative university). If a conventional college experience is truly not for you, then this is a great option to gain training in an alternate, but still intensive, way. These programs are also great for those who may hold a previous degree that did not adequately prepare them for the rigor of the professional world. There can be students from all ages in these programs and if you consider it a postsecondary option, it can be a really effective training tool.

Your List

Creating the "list" of schools you plan to audition for is arguably one of the most important steps in this process. Not only will it help keep you organized and grounded, but, if structured well, it can maximize your chances of getting accepted into a program. Only make a list of schools you would actually attend if you were accepted. Applying to a certain school because it is a popular and competitive school even though you aren't looking for a liberal arts–based education will make your list unnecessarily long and cam become a financial burden. Each school will have an application fee (can range from $50 to $100) and most will have an audition fee (typically around $50–$75). This process can become very expensive very quickly, and that is another reason you want to be thoughtful about your list.

Tip 3: Have about twelve to fifteen schools on your list.

Your list will most likely evolve over time as your research into each program deepens, so be flexible. But remember that with every application there is a fee. A wise recommendation suggests a list of seven to ten schools, separated into three categories: safety schools, match schools, and dream schools. While there is no real way to guarantee or quantify this, use the below definitions as a guide to help narrow down your list.

Safety Schools

These programs do not require auditions, and your grades and test scores will gain you admittance. These programs will typically be for a BA degree or have an audition after you arrive for placement within the class. Some of these programs might not be degree granting but will be a conservatory where you have the option of getting a degree. I would recommend at least having one safety school on your list.

Match Schools

According to Mary Anna Dennard, a college audition coach, these programs take more than 15 percent of those who audition, so your chances of acceptance are good but not guaranteed. Some factors that define a match school can include a larger incoming class size, a newer program, or fewer students auditioning. The majority of your acceptances will come from this list, so you want to include between six and eight of these schools.

Dream Schools

According to Dennard, these programs take fewer than 15 percent of those who audition. Programs like these will audition hundreds, sometimes thousands, of prospective students, while accepting a small freshmen class, often no more than thirty students. They are highly competitive and extremely popular. Consider having two to four dream schools on your list.

> **Tip 4:** Most top-tier performing arts programs accept less than 2 percent of those who audition. It is common for students to have a list filled with these amazing programs, as they are usually the most well known, the most sought out, and therefore highly competitive. In fact, most students interested in a BFA Musical Theater program will be auditioning for the same six to ten schools. But there are *many* other programs out there you may have never heard of that offer amazing Musical Theater educations. These schools may be easier to get into, as they can have a larger starting freshman class size, can have a bigger acceptance rate, can be an up-and-coming program, or do not require an audition. Make sure to flesh out your list with these match and safety schools. It is much more exciting to weigh the pros and cons of a handful of acceptances than to have no choices or options.

Chapter Takeaway

The Big Picture for a Big Process

It's only the beginning and you're already feeling overwhelmed. Don't worry: this process is manageable and you WILL get through to the other side. Here is a handy checklist to help you through these initial, important decisions.

- Create your team.

Even two can be a team! Find the person or people to help you navigate the application and audition process.

- Narrow down your program type.

Decide on the degree type and college experience that fit YOU.

- List your "other" preferences.

Consider the location, school size, housing options, and so on. Having a clear list to cross-reference will help you.

- Brainstorm school options.

As you find schools that appeal to you, divide them into dream, match, and safety schools.

- Finalize your list.

Be sure to have a few on either end of the spectrum, but with the majority of your schools falling into the best-fit/match schools. This number will be different for everyone.

- Get excited and inspired.

You've begun! Let's keep moving. . . . Remember that when things start to feel too big, or too complicated, break the task down to its most basic action steps and check them off, one at a time, as you go.

2 | "Summertime"
WAYS TO PREPARE

Take a deep breath, turn and look at your parents, friends, and family now and then, and realize they want what's best for you, but every hour of every day doesn't need to be consumed by your search for the perfect program, and how you're feeling at every moment along the way. Sometimes the universe sends you messages (like not even getting prescreened into your dream school), and that's a reality you might have to face. Let life happen to you while you're taking part in this process. Spend time with the people who care about you the most, but don't let the audition process monopolize the conversation.

—Catherine Weidner, Chair, Department of Theatre Arts, Ithaca College

Utilizing Your Summer

The summer between your junior and senior year of high school can be the perfect, and sometimes only, time to intensively prepare for the college audition process. Like everything else in this journey, there are many different paths you can take and there is no right or wrong way to do it. Even more important to state is that you don't need to spend the summer prepping in order to get into college. You don't. It can be incredibly beneficial, but it is not required.

There are many factors in how you spend your summers when you are in high school. Some are within your control, but many are not. You may need to work or take summer school or take a vacation with your family. You may volunteer or travel with a school group. Or, if you can, perhaps you spend the summer working on your craft.

If you are looking at a formal or more structured type of summer theater experience, then understand it will come with a price tag (although many summer programs will have scholarship opportunities). As with every decision in this process, it is important to first identify what you are looking for and then research the different ways you can meet those training needs.

> **Tip 1:** There is an entire industry of summer programs that cater to college audition preparation. Finding the right one for you could make all the difference in your level of preparedness and confidence.

Summer Programs

- Performing Arts Summer Camp

There is a wonderful tradition of performing arts sleepaway summer camps that exist all over North America. These specialized camps develop young talent—the campers—with the help of skilled counselors and faculty members, who conduct theater training and classes while providing a fun atmosphere of summer camp. The camps can offer courses in everything from Musical Theater, dance, acting, and voice, to circus skills, swimming, art, and even sports. Also, depending on the camp and how specialized in performing arts it is, there could be master classes taught by industry professionals and even college fairs where representatives from different universities are available for questions about the audition process for their departments. Sometimes you will be able to pick a "major," such as Musical Theater, acting, or voice, and a curriculum will be built around that. The camps also offer performance opportunities through full productions of existing musicals or in developing new work. Many of these focused camps have solid reputations for training young Musical Theater performers and preparing them for college auditions.

The goal of these camps is first and foremost fun, and students often start going as young as seven or eight years old, developing friendships and a community that last a lifetime. While the schedule and environment can often be rigorous, typically, that will align with the personality of a kid who is in love with the performing arts. The beauty of these types of camps is that they will balance all things performing arts with more traditional camp activities, such as hiking, camping, kayaking, or sports.

If you are not interested in such an intensive summer camp, you can look for camps that are less rigorous and use Musical Theater as a medium for encouraging fun, camaraderie, and creativity.

Money-Saving Tip 2: If you can, consider applying to be a counselor or counselor-in-training at one of these camps. This is a great way to make some money, gain leadership and employment experience, and have the opportunity to train while you work. In some of the more rigorous performing arts camps, this may not be an option, but for a regional camp that has some performing element, it could be a great way to get some experience while not spending a lot of money.

Tip 3: There are many wonderful camps to look at, but here are a few examples where you can begin you search: Stagedoor Manor, French Woods, Harand Camp of the Theatre Arts, and Perry Mansfield.

- On Campus

These type of programs strive to offer students a more concentrated training environment compared to most summer camps, while also preparing them to enter a professional Musical Theater career or theater training program at the college/preprofessional level. Typically these programs are shorter in length and focus only on college preparation.

Many universities with undergraduate Musical Theater departments or programs will have some kind of summer program on their campus. Some of these programs will be audition-based and some will not, but they will all cost money. These programs will give you a real sense of what it is like to be away from home, live in a dorm, eat in the cafeteria, and feel like a real college student. Most of the time these programs will be run or taught by the faculty of the program (though not always, because many faculty use the summer for their own professional development).

Some of these summer programs may conclude with an audition for the affiliated university's undergraduate Musical Theater program. This is an effective recruiting tool as it can save students the expense of having to fly back to the specific university at a separate time to go through the audition process. It will also give you a very good idea of whether you want to continue your education at that particular school. These types of summer programs can help to answer many of your questions about what to expect when you are in college and where you might fit best.

> **Tip 4:** It is really important to know that going to a precollege, on-campus program does not give you any kind of advantage when it comes to being accepted in that school's program.

- Intensives

Intensives are summer programs for young artists at an intermediate or advanced skill level, and these programs are typically not connected to a university or college. There are intensive programs for all ages around the country. Some are targeted to students as young as eight years old, but most intensives are focused on the high school population. Each of these programs typically lasts between one day and three weeks. Some intensives will be a combination of classes and preparation for a final show or showcase, while others will offer training exclusively. The faculty consists of working professionals in the field who are not usually connected to a university. Some of these programs will also have a college prep component for rising seniors, which can act as a crash course in audition preparation if needed.

> **Tip 5:** Programs to consider in this category are ArtsBridge, the Performing Arts Project (TPAP), Broadway Dreams Foundation, Broadway Artist Alliance, Open Jar, Broadway Theater Project, Making It on Broadway, the Broadway Workshop, Broadway Collective, and Summer Musical Theater Conservatory.

- Self-Directed Training

For those of you more inclined to take the nontraditional route, there are plenty of ways to spend your summer preparing for college Musical Theater programs. If you can identify an area of weakness in your training or an additional skill you'd like to learn while you have free time, creating your own summer curriculum could be a great and economical option. Search for voice lessons, beginning tap classes, acting seminars, or even a puppetry workshop in your area, and commit to attending all sessions. Or maybe you've spent your entire childhood devoted to all aspects of theater and could use a little break. Travel! Take a road trip to the next town over for the weekend, or a trip to the state park with great hiking. Go to a museum, watch classic films, try a new workout craze in your local gym, get a summer job, or even spend time with your family. We are always learning, one experience at a time, and that is not a bad way to spend a summer.

Chapter Takeaway

Sizzlin' Summer Study

Using dedicated time in the summer for additional Musical Theater training can really help take the pressure off your audition preparation during your senior year of high school, a busy time in its own right. If you leave the summer with a prescreen video, contrasting audition songs, monologue options, and a few practice auditions in front of professional artists and educators, you really will save yourself so much stress. Plus the experience of being away can also be beneficial (if you have not done that yet) in helping with the transition to life at college. However, the best aspect of summer Musical Theater study is the opportunity to create a really nice community of likeminded people who will soon be going through the same process together. This time and shared experience can build great friendships because you will have people you can lean on emotionally, and bounce ideas around with, as you research and prepare.

3 | "No One Is Alone"
THE AUDITION COACH

I do think it's valuable to work with a coach to assist in making audition choices.
A great coach can impart an amazing amount of advice and information to these
young artists that they would never know if preparing on their own! However,
I do think there can be, on occasion, such a thing as too much training so that
the work goes to their heads and it's so cerebral that their natural instincts are
muted. The gut and the very humanity of the material can get lost with too much
"brain."

—Gary Kline, Assistant Option Coordinator of Acting/Musical Theater,
Teaching Professor, Carnegie Mellon University

A S MORE AND MORE HIGH school students look to major in Musical
Theater, a real need has developed for families to seek out college
audition coaches or consultants to guide them. These are private
individuals or companies who take their clients step-by-step through the
audition process—think of it as a one-stop college audition prep shop.
These coaches will know the ins and outs of most programs, their current reputations, and what they offer to meet your individual needs as a
student. Many of these coaches have professional relationships with the
departments and their faculty, which can provide an intimate knowledge
of the university, curriculum, types of students, alumni, scholarships,
opportunities, school vibe, and so on.

I would say that roughly one-third of the students we see use a coach
or a coaching company to help them prepare for their college audition
(this is a very unscientific estimate). The growing competitive nature of
acceptances into BFA theater programs has helped to fuel this relatively

new cottage industry. Families have realized they need help navigating this process.

Good coaches will help you compile a realistic school application list, select appropriate songs and monologues for the auditions, organize your audition dates and what is required at each, help with audition attire, consult on résumés and headshot selection, and, in the end, help you make the final decision for the right program. They often hold mock auditions to help you become comfortable with auditioning in this format, and they facilitate master classes with program heads. Some coaches will accompany you to your audition, and others may also help with essays and SAT/ACT prep. Typically, relationships with these coaches start in the middle to end of junior year; however, if they still have room on their roster, they may take students as late as the middle of their senior year.

Many coaches work remotely, meaning you and your coach do not need to live in the same place, and most sessions happen over Skype or FaceTime, or a similar online platform. The bad news of this flexibility is that, at some point, you need to be in the same room. This can add to the overall cost of a coach if you need to travel to make that happen.

Tip 1: The bottom line is that college audition coaches are costly. If you cannot afford a coach but are determined to work with one, check to see if they offer any scholarships. Many coaches take on a few reduced or free students every season. Just be aware that even if you are a scholarship student, there are still many costs associated with a coach that may not be covered. Make sure you do your research and understand all the costs associated with their services before you sign up.

I think it is important to remember that your teachers and mentors have brought you this far—they know you as an artist and a whole person better than anyone. I encourage students to continue to work with trusted advisors and to seek their guidance as they navigate the college audition process. If additional master classes or individual lessons fill a void where a student desires enrichment, they should pursue it. I always encourage parents and students to carefully consider where they are spending their money, and what interest the person they are paying has at heart. Bottom line: is this relationship a healthy and good fit for you?

—Jason Debord, Assistant Professor of Music, Department
of Musical Theatre, University of Michigan

But Do I Need a Coach?

It is important to know that working with a coach will not give you any kind of advantage with the final outcome of acceptances. Talent, skill, and potential will get you accepted, regardless of whether you use a coach or not. A coach can (mostly) take the stress out of the process, especially for your team members, but that doesn't mean that everyone needs one. In fact, if you and your team have time to do the research and preparation, the savvy to keep everything organized and on track for all deadlines, and you follow this book (and others) as a guide, then you probably don't need a coach at all.

Ask yourself these questions to determine if you need a coach or not:

- Can I confidently navigate the process and understand all the different requirements?
- Do I, and/or a member of my team, have time to dedicate to completing all the steps involved with the application and audition processes?
- Do I have access to or know how to find the appropriate repertoire?
- Is there someone on my team I trust to guide me through difficult decisions?
- Can we afford it?

If all of your answers are "yes," perhaps you don't need a coach.

That decision is up to you, of course. Every person, family, and need is different.

The flip side to consider is the "overprepared" audition. I have seen many that are too controlled, too coached, and too "perfect." This can be a downfall of working with a coach, because of how specifically he or she can guide or direct your actual audition material. In these situations, we completely lose *you* and only see what you've been told to do and not do. This doesn't always happen, but it is something to consider. A good coach will insist that your individuality shines through, hopefully promoting your imperfect humanity and avoiding the robot version of you.

The subject of audition coaches is highly individual, both for you as the student and in how we, the adjudicators, see the final product. Here are a few other opinions about coaches that you can keep in mind when weighing the costs and benefits to you and your personal abilities:

A good audition coach can be very helpful for a student in choosing material, giving students a structure for their monologues, guiding them in technique, and giving them confidence. That said, it is important for me to be able to "play" with them and their acting choices to see if they can take direction and make adjustments. Holding onto the material too rigidly hinders an audition. We often accept students who have had no help and prior training at all.

—Barbara MacKenzie-Wood, Raymond W. Smith Professor of Acting, Carnegie Mellon University, School of Drama

In some students, working with a coach seems to help greatly refine their material and presentation. Unfortunately, in others it creates a polish and a performance slickness that is not what I am looking for at all. I wish there was a way to explain this to young people—that we are looking for skills, for sure, but not for so much polish that it is difficult to see the human in the performance.

—John Simpkins, Head of Musical Theatre, Penn State University

I do recommend that students get some qualified help in looking at their pieces, and coaches are increasingly part of the picture. I have found that some students who work with coaches are so polished that I can't tell if I'm really seeing them in their work or the coach. It can end up requiring a lot of digging to find the real person inside. I don't always have enough time to do that. Some students who've been highly coached are unable to make an adjustment because they're so locked into a performance.

—Joe Deer, Chair, Department of Theatre, Dance, and Motion Pictures, and Director of the Musical Theatre Initiative, Wright State University

Ask the Experts: Coaches in Their Own Words

To better understand what a college audition coach actually does, I want to introduce you to five wonderful coaches and have them explain what they do in their own words!

Mary Anna Dennard

Author of *I Got In* and *Before I Got In*

(These are great references, and I would recommend both books to you!)

I think of myself as an advocate for my students and families. What I do is guide them through the audition process. I help them navigate this complex

and intricate web of college performing arts applications and auditions. I find the programs and the schools that are going to give them what they want and need. I help them find their audition material—monologues and songs—if that is applicable. I help them learn how to define their type, how to know who they are as performers, and then show who they are in the audition room. I help them with scholarships and financial aid, and I ready them to be the best they can be, building their confidence so they go into the college audition process with joy and a feeling of high self-esteem. The college audition coach motto is "Be Joyous, because you love this; Be Brave, because you are fierce; Be Yourself, because you are enough."

Coaches are not cheap, but many families feel they are well worth the money. Parents might not blink at spending $1,000 for SAT prep. So, when the audition counts for as much as 80 percent in the admission process, why not spend your money on your audition prep? Expect to pay a coach $75 to $200 an hour. I would recommend that you find someone who is very experienced in this specific college audition process.

I do feel as though a coach can ease a lot of tension between parents and students; the audition process is complicated and stressful. A coach can actually save you money and heartache in the end—if you have been thoughtful and prepared in the way you approach the process—and in turn yield nice offers. Many families swear that having someone by their side who is familiar with the experience is a lifesaver.

Coaching students and guiding families is my bliss. We become very close. I am not just their coach: I am their advocate, mentor, best friend, teacher, therapist, and adopted mother. My work gives me more reward each and every year. But nothing gives me more happiness that when they call and say, "I got in!" That is the greatest reward of all.

Chelsea Diehl

Founder of *My College Audition*, author of *Before the College Audition*

As you may have heard, this career is not for the faint of heart. It requires an incredible amount of dedication and strength and a whole lot of passion. You, the prospective student, have made the decision to go to college to foster and develop this talent—but what is the right program for you? What are the odds of acceptance after an audition?

One of the essential reasons college audition coaches exist is to help answer these (and other) important questions. As a coach, I am able to watch you perform, assess your skill level, and help match you with programs that *will be an excellent fit for you as a performer and human being. I am able to accurately pinpoint reach, match, and safety performing arts schools that will give you the best odds of acceptance based on your skill set.*

Another valuable insight I like to instill with families right off the bat is that college auditions are not professional auditions. They want an exceptional human being who will contribute to their program and school. Confusing? Vague? Sure! But that's where we come in. Coaches are able to match you with fresh, powerful material (songs, monologues, dance combos) that best bring out all of the awesome qualities we have discovered about you while working together.

We also have the benefit of experience. We understand what these programs and their faculty are looking for and make it our goal to help you realize your full potential as both an artist and person.

And trust me on this one: it's much easier to hear from your coach that you need to devote more hours to practicing then to have your mother or father tell you to do so. We're happy to handle it. Audition coaching, when done correctly, should provide that best shot.

Halley Shefler

Founder of ArtsBridge Consulting

(ArtsBridge was founded in 2008 by Halley Shefler, who previously served as Dean of Admissions for the Boston Conservatory, as Director of Admissions for Boston University's College of Fine Arts School of Music, and as Director of Academic Affairs for the Longy School of Music.)

After experiencing the college admission process as an artist, admissions director, and parent, I found that student artists often do not receive the right advising during their college application process. Students have to find both the right artistic and academic match in a school, which is no simple task for a standard guidance counselor. In my years working in admissions, I observed that many students were applying to the wrong schools (sometimes not even getting in anywhere) because they lacked the proper guidance, so ArtsBridge Consulting was born.

ArtsBridge Consulting begins with the artistic assessment: two college faculty members with knowledge of admission standards review the client's artistic materials and provide the student with written, individualized feedback. This feedback is immensely helpful in determining where the student stands on the national artistic stage, and greatly informs the list of schools that students are advised to apply. Once artistic and academic levels are assessed, students are given a tailored college list on the ArtsBridge virtual college guide (which is constantly updated with new information and deadlines). The ArtsBridge team assists with every aspect of the application—essays, auditions, portfolio review, interview prep, and more—and support is provided to students and parents throughout every leg of the exciting and stressful application process.

Susan Woodell-Mascall

Founder of College Audition Pro

Navigating the college audition process can be daunting, intimidating, and just downright scary. This is especially true for families of first-time college applicants or families with no prior involvement in the performing arts. Hiring a college audition coach can help alleviate the stress and intensity of the journey.

Though a questionnaire, I help to identify the student's school list. Then we create "the Audition Material Package." I create a spreadsheet for each of my students with all the audition and prescreen requirements, as well as how, when, and where to sign up for the auditions. This is particularly helpful in "demystifying" how and when everything needs to be done in order to have a successful audition schedule.

As applications are completed and prescreen material submitted, I help my students create their résumés and recommend photographers to shoot their headshots and then help with the headshot selection and printing layouts.

Last year I merged my yearly individual workshops into my first "Summer University Theatre Experience" in San Francisco. Over two weeks my students worked with faculty from top Musical Theater and Acting programs. This invaluable experience allowed my students to learn from the best about the different programs and approaches.

In early January, I offer a mock audition to my students and I also hold a parent/student info session and go over how the Unified auditions run, how to handle "walk-in auditions," and what to bring. At our final session my students and I discuss the mock audition feedback and do a final run-through of the material before they head off to their first auditions!

When the acceptances, wait lists, and denials are received, I am there to advise and console. Denials are never easy, but, unfortunately, part of the process. Wait lists are very important and every year I have students accepted into the very top programs from wait lists. In the event of numerous acceptances, I encourage students to visit the schools and I connect them with my former students who are currently enrolled at the school.

Because my process is so labor- and time-intensive I try to limit my number of yearly contracted students to twenty-five. I do not audition, evaluate, or recruit students prior to working with them as I feel all students should have the opportunity to enlist the help of a coach. I have learned over the years how highly subjective this process is and every year I will be surprised that one student was accepted to a school and another was wait-listed or denied.

Ellen Lettrich

Founder of Musical Theater College Auditions (MTCA)

At MTCA, we guide each student and family through the artistic, organizational, and psychological processes of college auditions to fit their individual needs. We see our role as teachers and our students as emerging artists: we instill and develop foundational skills that lead to success in college auditions and beyond, while helping our students to discover the unique qualities and talents they have to share with schools.

MTCA helps guide you through the entire organizational part of this process. We start by helping students to formulate a comprehensive and diverse college list that matches their expressed interests and desires and gives them the best chance for success.

We then help them outline a rough coaching plan for the entire year that fits their schedule and budget. This covers where to focus training in various disciplines (depending on student needs), when to accomplish all the myriad items on the audition checklist (prescreens, headshots, etc.), when and where to schedule auditions, and more. Throughout the year, we check in with each student on their organizational progress and help them accomplish their timeline goals. This process has become more and more difficult to navigate over the years, and while some of our students come in with a strong organizational plan and are able to stick to it (which we encourage!), many students and parents will lean on our years of experience as it all becomes overwhelming.

Psychologically, the benefits of using a coaching team like MTCA can be hugely impactful. This can be such a whirlwind of a process and very difficult to go through alone. MTCA helps families both by offering strategic ideas to mitigate psychological challenges throughout their audition journey and by being there to share stories of our years of experience as professionals in the business and as coaches for the college process. We know how to help students get into the most productive mind-frame for their big auditions and throughout the long process of waiting for admission results.

Chapter Takeaway

The Pros and Cons of an Audition Pro

Are you still weighing whether an audition coach is right for you? Here is a concise list of things to consider.

Pros

- This is what a coach does professionally. It is not their first audition process. They are experts.
- Coaches will often have a relationship with many schools so they know the inside details of those programs, thus being able to find a good fit for you.
- Many coaches will have master classes with heads of programs.
- Many coaches will provide mock auditions to help you practice.
- They will give an honest first impression of you and your talent and help to make an appropriate college list for you.
- They are an encyclopedia of repertoire and material for songs and monologues.
- They will help prep your résumé, tell you what to wear, and keep you organized.
- You can meet other students in their "class" and share experiences and struggles.
- Your team can meet others going through the process too.
- They will be there to guide and coach you through every step of the process.
- You have a built-in cheerleading team. They are rooting for your success.

Cons

- The price tag. Coaching services can be very expensive.
- The price tag.
- The price tag.
- The (possible) restriction of location and face-to-face opportunities.
- The too-polished package. Some students become too mechanical and slick because of the amount of coaching/overcoaching.
- The too similar package. Some coaches create a "look" for all their students that is too similar and doesn't allow your personality to shine through.

4 | "Sing Me a Happy Song"
AUDITION SONGS

Potential students are used to hearing advice such as "be yourself," "we just want to see who you are," and so forth. "Being yourself" can be a challenge for a young person, particularly because he or she may want to become an actor so that they can be someone else! The important thing for us is that the student performs selections they can relate to, that come from plot-driven musicals (not revues), and consist of roles that could conceivably be played by the person auditioning. Creating a "reality" is important, as is singing about something the singer really needs or wants. Of course, excellent technique helps!

—Roger Grodsky, Professor, Music Director, and Vocal Coach, University of Cincinnati College-Conservatory of Music (CCM)

Audition Requirements

At your audition, you will most often be asked to present two contrasting musical theater songs. Those songs will usually come from two distinct categories: Golden Age (they may use the words "classic," "traditional," or "standard") and contemporary. They may also distinguish your songs further by asking for a "ballad" and an "up tempo." Each program you audition for will have very specific requirements that may differ slightly, so be sure to have a clear way to keep that information organized as you prepare.

Rarely will you have the opportunity to sing a full song in your college audition (though you should know the whole thing in case you are asked for it). In most instances, you will be asked to sing a "cut" of these songs that is either 16 or 32 bars in length, or you will be given a specific time limit. Cutting your songs down requires musical and dramatic skill, so it is best to ask a pianist or vocal coach who knows the repertoire how to help you as cut needs to make both musical and dramatic sense (for more help with cuts and song selection from the pianist/accompanist perspective, see chapter 9). There are songbooks and websites like *Music Notes* out there that already have cuts prepared, so you can look into those as well.

Tip 1: I am going to be listing lots of song examples in this chapter. Please take the time to listen to them as it can not only enhance your own repertoire knowledge, but also help you identify the specifics of what works and why.

Tip 2: A general rule of thumb is that 32 bars should be between 1:00 and 1:30 minutes long. A 16-bar cut is between 30 and 45 seconds long. Chapter 9 provides more help regarding audition cuts.

Tip 3: No matter the length of the cut, your song must tell a complete story.

Let's now explore the meanings for some of the words that are used to describe songs.

- Contrasting

This means that the style, feel, tempo, genre, and/or where it fits in the voice is *opposite* from the other song you choose. For example, "It Only Takes a Moment" from *Hello Dolly!* and "Dancing through Life" from *Wicked.* Those two songs are different from each other in genre, tempo, and style.

- Ballad and Up Tempo

This refers to the speed of your song. Simply put, ballad = slower and up tempo = faster. "If I Loved You" from *Carousel* = ballad; "Try Me" from *She Loves Me* = up tempo.

- Golden Age/Standard/Classic/Traditional

Many different words can be used here, but basically we are talking about theatrical songs that were written from the turn of the century to 1965. Though they are similar, each term has some distinguishing features:

- The *Golden Age* of musical theater is most often defined as musicals that were written between 1943 and 1965. Most Golden Age songs are *character driven*, meaning that a character in a musical sings about a very specific moment that is related to the plot. In Golden Age material, we are looking for how you understand the style of the period vocally and dramatically.
- A *standard* refers to material written between 1920 and 1940 and, by definition, were pop songs of the era. These songs were often never in or written for a traditional musical (though some were and some were later put into musicals). Some were written for movies, some for a singer to perform on TV or in a solo-type of show, and some were written as stand-alone songs for radio. "How Deep Is the Ocean" by Irving Berlin is an example and an excellent audition song.

Tip 4: I know that you will have audition requirements that will state that your audition songs must be from a musical. Some of the most well-known standards were ultimately not put into musicals per se, but the strong majority were written by theater composers. I think standards work great for college auditions because they are beautifully written songs with lyrics that are actable through a variety of interpretations. I have trouble believing that anyone at your audition will care that your standard (if you choose to sing one) was not originally written for a character in a musical. Irving Berlin, who wrote many standards, is a theater composer: his songs are all structured like a song that belongs in a musical, and they have clear objectives and obstacles (which will be explained later in this chapter). This is only my opinion, but I say go for it if you love the song.

Tip 5: If you choose to sing a standard, you have the responsibility of giving the song a story or point of view because it inherently won't come with a plot behind the song.

Tip 6: Check out composers such as Harold Arlen, Cole Porter, Ira and George Gershwin, and Irving Berlin when you are looking for songs in the standard repertoire.

- Contemporary

These are songs from musicals written *after* 1965. There are many subcategories here, but this is the general term that is used. Composers range from Stephen Sondheim to Kander and Ebb, Andrew Lloyd Webber to Jason Robert Brown, and beyond. What is crucial is that they are from musicals and **not** from movies or pop/rock/R&B songs.

> **Tip 7:** If you do decide to sing a contemporary song that is not from a musical, always have additional material that *is* from a musical in case they want to hear that as well. We see these songs a lot. They are typically stand-alone songs that were written to be performed in a cabaret or concert.
>
> **Tip 8:** Do not sing a pop/rock/R&B song unless there are specific instructions that say it is acceptable.
>
> **Tip 9:** In some instances, pop/rock/R&B songs that *have* been put into musicals are acceptable, but pick wisely as they typically are not as easily actable. If you use a song in this category, make sure you use the arrangement from the show. Some examples are songs from shows like *All Shook Up*, *Rock of Ages*, and *Xanadu*.

Choosing Your Songs

The perfect song allows you to focus on the acting while showing us what you are capable of vocally. A successful song never shows us notes that you almost have, it only shows us what you do have. Keep it short and simple, you want to leave us wanting more.

—Matt Edwards, Associate Professor and Coordinator of Musical
Theatre Voice, Shenandoah University

> **Tip 10:** When choosing your audition songs (and monologues), it is very important to understand that if you are Caucasian, it is not appropriate to sing material specifically written for a character of color.

Following the guidelines below should take a lot of stress out of the idea of finding the "perfect" song and help you find material that will make you feel confident, comfortable, and at ease, like you are wearing a gown or suit that was tailor-made just for you! There is endless material out there. Don't settle. Just like everything else in this process, the material you pick teaches us about you, so be very thoughtful about this piece of the equation. Also see tables 4.1 and 4.2, for song ideas for a particular gender.

When looking for your audition material, find songs that . . .

- You *love* and *connect to.*

If you love to sing your song, that will show in your audition. And if you relate to and understand what the character wants, it can make your acting choices stronger.

- You are really, really good at *right now.*

If you choose material that is out of your reach vocally or emotionally, or that exposes an area of your skill that lacks confidence, then it has the real potential of taking the auditors out of your moment and may have us wondering why you didn't find something that fit better.

- Are *bulletproof.*

Meaning songs you can sing no matter how you feel—sick, healthy, tired, or nervous.

> *A good song is one the auditioning student can relate to, where they can create an understanding of the lyrics. Also, a song that he/she can sing when first starting the day: do not try a song that you've only hit the high notes once in a voice lesson.*
>
> —Mark Madama, Associate Professor of Musical Theatre, University of Michigan

- Are in the *sweet spot of your voice.*

There is no need to show us every part of your voice in this audition; there is just not enough time. And no matter what you *think* we want or need to hear, I want to tell you specifically that we want to hear your *best*. If you are offering songs that contrast in where they sit in your voice, make sure that each is still confident in its placement. For example, if you don't belt yet . . . don't belt. If your legit is not strong . . . don't show us that.

- Are in your *dramatic range.*

You want to pick material that you can authentically interpret. This can vary greatly depending on your personal experience and ability, but you want to find material that you truly understand and can present with confidence and authenticity. It will give us the opportunity to *see you* and your potential, and in some instances truly meet you for the very first time.

> *A song is successful in the audition room if it is sung well and if the performer understands what they are singing about. If the performer allows the song to affect them physically, emotionally, and imaginatively, that's a bonus because it indicates a kind of freedom and the singer is not worrying about the high note or listening to how they sound.*
>
> —Tracey Moore, Professor, The Hartt School,
> Theatre Division, University of Hartford

- Allow you to be *in your body.*

One of the things that many schools will look for in assessing your ability is how comfortable you are in your own skin, as well as how you use and are connected to your body. This means that you understand what "neutral" is and that you have no identifiable tics—rubbing your fingers together, touching your dress or pants, conducting with one of your arms, and so on. Everything starts from a neutral place, but each song should have a different physicality because the music, lyric, time period, and point of view will all be different. Musical Theater is a heightened art form and sometimes requires a physical life that is bolder and more activated than you may think. Do your research and watch, watch, watch how professionals use their bodies. See how an actor's behavior changes depending on the kind of song they are singing.

Let's break down these ideas of choosing a *good-fit-for-you* song with a specific example:

> "I Could Have Danced All Night" from *My Fair Lady* is a classic and strong Golden Age up tempo for a soprano. It is also a song that sits high in the female voice, is sustained, is technically difficult to sing, and can be challenging for a young singer. The song is for an advanced legit soprano. So, the auditioner starts with "I Could Have Danced All Night," and it is weak and breathy, the vibrato is fluttery, and the whole thing is unstable. Could be nerves, could be lack of technique, or could be that it is just out of their technical reach. As the auditor I think, "this is not going well," and my first impression is that maybe you are not skilled enough to make it to the "yes" pile. I am disappointed because I love what you are offering as an actor. Then your second piece, "Journey to the Past" from Anastasia

is brilliant. The song sits in the sweet spot of your voice, you are emotionally connected to the material, and dramatically, you take us on a thrilling ride. After you are done, I ask why you chose the first song (a question I often ask). You say that your voice teacher wanted you to show the potential you have in your legit sound. This is like saying that you are willing to go to a job interview as a writer with grammatical errors in your writing sample. Look, *our job is to see your potential.* That is what we do every day, and we are really, really good at it. *I can't say this strongly enough: Do not sing in a part of your range that isn't strong because you think you should.*

If a teacher gives you a song you don't connect with or one that you are skeptical about singing with confidence no matter what, don't sing it. I understand that you may feel like you are hurting the feelings of the person that is guiding you but this process is about you, not them. I know this can be hard to hear because you have paid a lot of money and put a lot of trust into the people who are helping you, and please understand I do not mean don't listen to them or that you know better. What I am saying is that if the song is not something you can nail (vocally and dramatically) every time, then you simply should choose something else. Find songs that resonate in your voice, body, and soul. If the song you have been given doesn't feel right, then it is your responsibility to speak up! The canon of repertoire is endless so don't settle. Plus, looking for material to sing at your auditions should excite you like crazy, not overwhelm you. Think of your research for great material as the beginning of your professional training. This is the most fun research assignment you have ever been given!

What if, in that example above, for a Golden Age up tempo you sing, "If I Were a Bell" from *Guys and Dolls* instead of "I Could Have Danced All Night." It is still legit and Golden Age, but it doesn't sit too terribly high in the voice. It shows musical control but has a lot of room for interpretation, and we love hearing it.

Another Perspective on Choosing Your Songs

Gary Kline, Assistant Option Coordinator of Acting/Musical Theater, Teaching Professor, Carnegie Melon University

- *The song must have a personal connection to the person singing it. It should feel like the singer wrote the lyric. The song should fit like* the proverbial glove! When the young person singing the song can not only identify with the material but also inhabit it, the moments become something quite special while watching and listening.

- The melody must be within EASY grasp of the singer's vocal skills and range without pushing or straining. Who wants to watch you sweat by working too hard to sing a song that is out of your reach?

- Musically, there should be moments of true "sustain" so that one can hear the vocal quality. A vocal (and emotional) climax is a good idea. The "money note" should not be eschewed. It can express a very powerful inner emotional life if truly sung from the core of one's needs.

- Generally, the "esoteric" songs do not make good song choices. Simple is always better! Complicated and unknown songs generally leave me scratching my head about the content of the song, and can also truly tick off the pianist. I find myself wondering what show it's from, where it is going, and who wrote it, instead of truly listening to the singer. Don't leave me puzzled by your "clever" choice.

- Character songs might be best reserved for specific auditions for a particular show, or perhaps used in a cabaret. Please remember, I am not casting a show! Playing the character as done in the show is futile when I'm trying to figure out who you are and if I want to invite you in as part of an MT class where I will spend four years with you. The song should be personal and transparent so I can see through the material into **you**!

- A song sung in a "character voice" or accent is a waste of my time, as I cannot divine the singer's true voice—"Just You Wait," "I Cain't Say No," etc. Keep it real, please. Your speaking and singing voices should not be drastically different.

- Singing songs written for life experiences of the more mature, older actor cannot possibly represent the young seventeen-year-old singer to their best advantage. Examples: "Your Daddy's Son" "Rose's Turn," "What Did I Have That I Don't Have," "Stars," "Falcon in the Dive." Stay in your age and vocal lane!

- Also, why sing a victim song or a song that looks backward when there are so many great "I want"/"I wish" songs that look toward the future?

- Belting (mainly for women) as high and as loud as one can is not a way to impress. There are songs that have been "screamed" for years, like "Shy," "Johnny One Note," "Gimme Gimme," that have *no personal connection to the young singer. They are only about volume, and that is never impressive.*

- *Confidence is attractive. Don't enter with an apology. Be brave enough to make your private moments public by releasing your pain and pleasures in an unsheltered place. Now that takes confidence, and, man, is it attractive!*

Song Types

A successful song is one where the artist has a personal connection and specific dramatic circumstance at work in the material. It is easy to adjudicate a healthy voice and trained singing. What makes a musical theatre performer truly successful is the unique way they choose to move through their circumstance—how powerful, how specific, how personal are they willing to be? This tells me volumes about how they will be to work with in class or rehearsal.

—John Simpkins, Head of Musical Theatre, Penn State University

I am often asked whether we have a "do not sing" list. The quick answer is that most schools don't (more from my fellow colleagues below). However, make sure you look at the audition requirements to be sure. Of course, there are songs that I love to hear and others that I would rather not hear again, but every person's approach to the work and the material is unique, so I believe that you could be the person to change my mind.

Song Types That Work Well

- Songs That Are Immediately Actable

Right away, the lyrics of such a song take you and us on a journey that has an objective and obstacle (see the definitions later in this chapter). These are songs where the character has a clear need or want and is often ready to take action by the end.

- Songs That You Connect to Personally

These are songs where the lyric tells the story of something that either directly relates to you or makes you feel empathy for the situation. A song about first love would fit into this category.

- Songs That Sit in the "Sweet Spot" of Your Voice

These are songs that you can SIINNGG with ease and confidence. For example, if you are a soprano with a really solid and exciting high G, then "I'll Know" from *Guys and Dolls* just may be in the sweet spot of your voice.

- Songs That Make You Feel Powerful and Grounded

These are songs that have an empowered lyric or a powerful message.

- Songs That Are Written for People Your Age

There is countless material written for young people. Some show titles include *Bring It On, Heathers, Legally Blonde, Flora the Red Menace, Oklahoma!,* and *In the Heights.*

- Songs That Exude Joy

This is a great way for us to first meet someone in an audition. Typically, these songs are not only age-specific, but they tend to come with a sensibility that stems from gratitude and that can work very well.

- Songs That Can Teach Us about You in Some Way

Are you a guy that loves rock music and is funny? Then look at "Goodbye and Good Luck" from *High Fidelity.* Are you tenor and a passionate romantic? Then look at "Love to Me" from *Light in the Piazza.* Are you a high-energy, bubbly belter with good comedic chops? Then look at "Anything" from *Triumph of Love.*

> *Auditions to me are about finding songs that show off your skill sets and range, to be sure, but also contain a positive personal connection. Be the lens through which the material is seen. That way I get to know YOU while I see if the other pieces are in place.*
>
> —Danny Gurwin, Division Head, Musical Theatre,
> Co-Chair, Acting/Musical Theatre, University of Arizona

- Songs That Are about Change or Embarking on Something New

These kinds of songs are also a great way to be introduced to a prospective student. They tend to have musical drive and a real discovery within them.

- Songs That Have an Epiphany in Them

Oprah describes this as an "ah-ha" moment—where a light bulb clicks on and from that moment on you are different.

- Songs about Helping Other People in Some Way

These songs have inherent obstacles in them.

Song Types That Do Not Work as Well

- Songs That Have Repetitive Lyrics and Notes

Why waste your cut on the same notes over and over?

- Songs about an Experience That You Cannot Relate To

It's best to find songs that are from the point of view of someone your age and experience.

- Songs That Are a "Pity Party" or Tell Us That You "Suck"

You have such little time in your audition, why would you choose a lyric that, simply put, makes you look bad? With so much material out there, there is no need to pick something that is self-defeating. I do find that young actors gravite to these songs because they have lots of "feelings" in them. Feelings are not acting. Understand the difference.

- Songs That Are Out of Your Range or Vocal Style

Are you a legit soprano who has not learned how or is not yet confident in your belt? Then don't choose the contemporary up tempo "I'm Not" from *Little by Little*. Choose something you can sing in the mix (or middle) part of your voice instead. Something like "Dancing All the Time" from *Big* or "Spark of Creation" from *Children of Eden*.

- Songs That Don't Have a Dramatic Narrative

These are songs where the lyric is abstract and doesn't have an easily interpretable story or direction. Interpreting sung poetry is an advanced skill and even though the songs might be age-appropriate, they truly don't work in a college audition format because of the lack of direct narrative.

- Songs That Are "High Comedy"

This can be a piece that is overtly character-driven in a way that makes it about the song instead of about the actor. Rarely does this type of song work in the college audition setting because it can be difficult to see you through the song. More often than not, the songs themselves can outshine or overpower you.

- Songs That Have Nonwords in Them

Since you have such a brief time in the audition, we need lyrics to help see your ability to tell a story.

- Songs That Are Classical Arias or from an Operetta (Unless Asked)

Please read the requirements carefully, and if it doesn't specifically ask for an aria or a song from an operetta, then, simply put, . . . don't sing one. If this is what you do best and you are set on singing it, then ask the auditors if they would be interested in hearing it before you just jump right in, and always have a backup in case they say no.

> **Tip 11:** The exception to this rule is if you are auditioning for a BMus degree. In this case, you will almost certainly be asked for a classical piece.

- The Newest, Coolest Song That No One Has Heard

Most programs support and love new writers and new works, but your college audition is not necessarily the right place for this material. If the auditors are hearing a song for the first time, you run a great risk that they are listening to the song and not you.

> **Tip 12:** This is where your research will really help you. If you know that a particular school is a champion of new work and has composers on faculty, they may be more open to hearing songs that were written in the last few years, as they may already know them.

- Songs That Need You to Have a Lisp or Accent

Most songs that have a lisp or an accent in the show's context can be done in an audition setting without it. We want to hear your natural voice.

- Songs That Identify You as Crazy

Why introduce yourself to us with a song that is about an emotionally unstable person?

- Songs That Tell Me You Are A STAR

I am sure you are, but let us be the judge of that.

- Songs That Are Overtly Sexual

It is just not the right place for it, no matter how liberal the school.

Songs are most successful when the artist is aligned with the material. Thorough preparation, age appropriate material choice, and secure demonstration of the individual's skill set—no aspirational notes please. Artists who bring thorough preparedness will be in charge of their audition, and thereby leaving room for discovery in the moment.

—Hank Stratton, Assistant Professor, Acting/MT Division, University of Arizona

---

Tip 13: Standards can make great gender-neutral song options if you want to go that route. We LOVE hearing these songs in the room. They are easy to cut, the pronouns are interchangeable, the songs are actable, and oh so beautiful. A few examples of great standards: "All The Things You Are"—Jerome Kern, "The Nearness of You"—Hoagy Carmichael, "What'll I Do"—Irving Berlin, "My Romance"—Richard Rodgers and Lorenz Hart, "Love Is Here to Stay"—George and Ira Gershwin, and "Here I'll Stay"—Kurt Weill.

Please select material that best suits your gender at the time of your audition. If you are gender-fluid or non-binary, then select material that best reflects the stories you want to tell or roles you want to play. Remember, your song choices help us meet you and therefore, choosing material that reflects who you are is not only helpful, but incredibly important.

TABLE 4.1. Examples of Songs That Work Well and Why for Male-Identified Applicants

SONG	SHOW	CATEGORY	REASON
"Lost in the Wilderness"	*Children of Eden*	Contemporary tenor, up tempo	Clear scene partner, clear obstacle, lots of excitement and visceral energy.

(continued)

TABLE 4.1. Continued

SONG	SHOW	CATEGORY	REASON
"Streets of Dublin"	*A Man of No Importance*	Contemporary, bari-tenor, up tempo	World of the song is very clear and has great energy and drive (but no need for the accent).
"Something's Coming"	*West Side Story*	Golden Age, bari-tenor, up tempo	It is joyous, open, and passionate.
"Issue in Question"	*Triumph of Love*	Contemporary, tenor, up tempo	Has a great obstacle and a great epiphany (ah-ha moment).
"Take a Chance on Me"	*Little Women*	Contemporary, tenor, up tempo	Hopeful and open. Requires fun tactics. Has a clear obstacle.
"Out There"	*Hunchback of Notre Dame*	Contemporary, tenor, power ballad	Clear obstacle and objective. Hopeful.
"Let It Sing"	*Violet*	Contemporary, bari-tenor, up tempo	Song is about cheering someone up.
"I Made a Fist"	*The Most Happy Fella*	Golden Age, tenor, up tempo	This song is empowered and is about standing up for something for the first time.
"Big, Bright, Beautiful World"	*Shrek*	Contemporary, bari-tenor, up tempo	Open, joyous with a strong obstacle.
"Lucky to Be Me"	*On the Town*	Golden Age, baritone, ballad	Open, joyous, and youthful.
"She Loves Me"	*She Loves Me*	Golden Age, bari-tenor, up tempo	Open, joyous, and youthful.
"Try Me"	*She Loves Me*	Golden Age, bari-tenor, up tempo	Open, joyous, and youthful.
"Boy with Dreams"	*Edges*	Contemporary, tenor, up tempo	Open, joyous, and youthful.
"Miracle of Miracles"	*Fiddler on the Roof*	Golden Age, bari-tenor, up tempo	Open, joyous, and youthful.
"Love to Me"	*Light in the Piazza*	Contemporary, bari-tenor, up tempo	Open, joyous, and youthful.
"Everybody Says Don't"	*Anyone Can Whistle*	Golden Age, bari-tenor, up tempo	Great obstacle and objective.
"Goodbye and Good Luck"	*High Fidelity*	Contemporary, bari-tenor, up tempo	Funny, human, honest.

TABLE 4.2. Examples of Songs That Work Well and Why for Female-Identified Applicants

SONG	SHOW	CATEGORY	REASON
"Love Don't Turn Away"	*110 in the Shade*	Golden Age, mix/legit, ballad	This song is about discovery and the lyric asks questions that make the song very active.
"Hand in Hand"	*By Kerrigan and Lowdermilk*	Contemporary, mix/legit	Song is full of joy and discovery.
"Anything"	*Triumph of Love*	Contemporary, belt, up tempo	Has a clear and urgent objective. Can be funny.
"Before It's Over"	*Dogfight*	Contemporary, mix, ballad	Immediate and full of hope and wonder.
"Stranger to the Rain"	*Children of Eden*	Contemporary, mix, ballad	Strong objective and obstacle. Age-appropriate.
"I Hate the Bus"	*Caroline or Change*	Contemporary, mix ballad	Strong objective and obstacle. Age-appropriate.
"Women"	*The Pirate Queen*	Contemporary, mix/belt, power ballad	Strong and empowered. Immediately actable.
"Sing Happy"	*Flora the Red Menace*	Golden Age, belt, (ballad or up tempo depending on the cut)	Strong and empowered. Immediately actable.
"Get Out and Stay Out"	*9–5*	Contemporary, high belt, up tempo	Strong and empowered. Immediately actable.
"On My Way"	*Violet*	Contemporary, mix/belt, up tempo	On the precipice of something new. Full of joy.
"Life I Never Led"	*Sister Act*	Contemporary, mix/belt, ballad	Great obstacle and objective.
"Is It Really Me"	*110 in the Shade*	Golden Age, mix, ballad	Great epiphany and clear scene partner.
"Piece of Sky"	*Yentl*	Contemporary, mix/belt/ballad	Joyous and full of discovery.
"I'll Know"	*Guys and Dolls*	Golden Age, soprano, ballad	Strong, clear scene partner, immediate.

Be different. We hear so much material from what is currently playing on Broadway. When an auditioning student comes in and sings a song with their own added style, it is clear to me who they are as an artist. If you have a country sound, sing some country. If you have a rock voice and love rock, sing rock!

—Robin Lewis, Associate Professor for Musical Theatre/Dance, Rider University

For songs that don't work as well in the audition room and why, see table 4.3.

TABLE 4.3. Songs That Don't Work as Well in the Audition Room and Why

SONG	SHOW	REASON
"Any Dream Will Do"	*Joseph and the Amazing Technicolor Dreamcoat*	Repetitive notes and lyrics.
"I'm Still Here"	*Follies*	Lyric is for someone much older with extensive life experience.
"But Not for Me"	*Crazy for You*	Why would you spend your audition time telling us that you suck?
"Nobody Does It Like Me"	*Seesaw*	
Anything from Spring Awakening	*Spring Awakening*	It is hard to find a dramatic narrative in the lyric here. These songs are sung poetry and thus very challenging to interpret in audition cuts.
"I'm Not That Smart"	*Spelling Bee*	High comedy.
"Betrayed"	*The Producers*	
"My New Philosophy"	*You're A Good Man, Charlie Brown*	
"Purpose"	*Avenue Q*	The cut has too many "nonliteral" words such as "ba da ba."
"Screw Loose"	*Cry Baby*	This song identifies you as crazy. Not the impression you want to make.
"I'm the Greatest Star"	*Funny Girl*	Best to avoid songs that tell us you are A STAR.
"I'm a Star"	*By Scott Allen*	
"Dead Girl Walking"	*Heathers*	These songs are too overtly sexual.
"A Call from the Vatican"	*Nine*	
"Pulled"	*Addams Family*	Simply because this was one of the most sung songs in the past few years.

Note: I am not telling you not to sing these. They are great songs, but having sat through thousands of auditions, I can tell you why these types of songs are not as effective. Perhaps the key is finding the ideal cut, but these examples can be difficult to be successful with.

> **Tip 14:** Remember that all of this is *very subjective*. What one school likes to hear may not be what another school likes. There is no real way for you to know this, and it will make you crazy trying to figure that out or make everyone happy. If there is a song listed in the "does not work as well" section that is so you and encapsulates everything you are and want to show, then I say go for it. You just need to understand the pitfalls before committing to it.

"Do Not Sing" Lists

Let's chat about this topic a little more. Most schools will *not* have a "do not sing" list. But as you will see below, this topic is very subjective in how each of us reacts to the overused, unknown, or often poorly executed songs, and it is hard to give general "advice" for this topic. I'm going to let my fellow colleagues speak for themselves. (This really is invaluable advice to consider when choosing your material.)

> *I do not have a "do not sing" list. There are certainly things I want to hear less than others—for a million reasons, most of which have to do less with my affection for a particular song and more with how some songs are more difficult to adjudicate in the audition room because of their subject matter, style, mannerisms, or affects. But I feel stronger that artists should be given the benefit of preparing the things about which they are passionate. Sometimes an actor sings a song that would be on my "do not sing" list— but they do it in a way that approaches it individually and with a freshness that I haven't previously seen. In that instance, if I had a "do not sing" list, I would have lost the opportunity to experience that artist in their chosen material. Plus, if they do something that is difficult for me to adjudicate, I'll always ask for something else or go looking in their audition book for additional material.*
>
> —John Simpkins, Head of Musical Theatre, Penn State University

> *There is no "list" that we publish, but we do have a lot of songs we are tired of hearing. Again, we don't want to make this any harder for the students than it already is. However, doing an overdone song does come with a cost and it is in the student's best interest to do their research and avoid them. Using an overdone song makes us think you are not serious enough to do the research to find great material that is not overdone. It also sets you up*

to be compared to everyone else who has sung that song instead of being evaluated on just your performance.

—Matt Edwards, Associate Professor and Coordinator of Musical
Theatre Voice, Shenandoah University

The "do not sing" list is on our website. The list is made up of songs agreed on by the faculty that we find to be not helpful in getting the information we need. Most of them got on there because we were seeing them a lot, and we felt the song choices did not serve the students in an audition context for colleges. This doesn't mean we don't love the songs; they just are not beneficial for us to get what we need.

—Kaitlin Hopkins, Head of Musical Theatre, Texas State University

There's no hard rule on this, but I suppose my "do not sing" list includes the obvious infractions: "Astonishing" and "Defying Gravity." The expectation is simply too high for both of these songs, and the context of an audition rarely supports these choices. There is so much material to choose from, why undermine your audition by insisting on singing contemporary work so encumbered by enormous technical challenges and our memory of its original performance? I suppose though, like everything, time and distance may return these songs to the canon.

—Hank Stratton, Assistant Professor, Acting/Musical Theater Division,
University of Arizona

I'm happy to hear what the student does well and has passion for. There are certainly songs I don't need to hear at auditions anymore, or at least right now. But, I don't hold that against a student and would never penalize them for that.

—Joe Deer, Chair, Department of Theatre, Dance, and Motion Pictures,
and Director of the Musical Theatre Initiative, Wright State University

We do not have a do-not-sing list. In my personal view, it is not up to me to say that a student cannot find an interpretive aspect to a song that I have not previously seen. I encourage students to pick a piece that is age-appropriate, shows us specific acting and interpretive choices, and shows the panel the finest aspects of their musical abilities.

—Jason Debord, Assistant Professor of Music,
Department of Musical Theatre, University of Michigan

We do not. "Overdone" songs tend to have bad reputations because they are poorly done. Your song choices tell me numerous things about your skill, experience, training, perspective, and teachability. Every song choice is a risk in some way.

—Danny Gurwin, Division Head, Musical Theatre, Co-Chair,
Acting/Musical Theatre, University of Arizona

Tracks

If you are auditioning on campus, then you can almost always plan on having live accompaniment. If you are auditioning at Unifieds (explained in chapter 8) or at a venue that is not on campus, then there is a very good chance that you will be singing with a recorded track. This means that you sing your audition cuts from prerecorded accompaniment.

Since each school has different requirements, you will need to have tracks ready for each cut of every song. This can be an additional expense that you will need to factor in if you are not working with someone who can record the tracks for you. There are many theater pianists that will record for you no matter where you are, and a quick Google search will help you identify them. All you need to do is email them a PDF of your music with your cuts perfectly marked and they will send you MP3s back.

Most schools will not accept you singing a cappella. A cappella means singing without any accompaniment. You never want to do this because, simply put, you are not auditioning for *American Idol.* Musical theater is a collaborative art form, and the relationship with the music that is written to support the melody is part of what makes the song possible.

If you are singing with recorded accompaniment, then you should assume that you need to bring speakers into the room with you to play your tracks. The key to this situation is being organized and keeping your setup very low maintenance. Ideally, your speakers should be wireless and charged so nothing needs to be plugged in. A Bluetooth connection is usually best, if possible. Also consider what your tracks are going to be played from: your phone, iPad, MP3 player? Make sure you turn off all of your notifications and have immediate access to the songs so you are not fumbling in the room.

Have each song on a different track that is clearly marked for you to quickly find what you need. For example: "I'm Here" (16-bar cut).

> **Tip 15:** Practice setting up your tracks numerous times. You don't want to be fumbling in the room, so rehearsing the setup will help. If fumbling does happen, don't stress or panic. It is a great opportunity to show who you are in how you solve the issue. No need to overly apologize. Just get the problem worked out.

Your Audition Book

In addition to your two contrasting pieces that you have been asked to prepare, you may also be asked for something else from your "book." This is the binder with all your performable material that you give to the accompanist. Make sure that you only have songs in your book that you are fully prepared to sing in an audition. Sometimes if I want to see more, I will take a flip through your book to see what I might like to hear, so it is in your best interest to have your book hyper-organized, with a table of contents or a list of songs in the front. You will want to have at least five different songs ready to use in any audition:

- Golden Age/Standard Up Tempo

A quick moving theatrical song that is written before 1965.

- Golden Age/Standard Ballad

A slower moving theatrical song that is written before 1965.

- Contemporary Up Tempo

A quick moving song from a musical that is written after 1965.

- Contemporary Ballad

A slower moving song from a musical that is written after 1965.

- Pop/Rock/Country/R&B

(ONLY if that is what you do) OR something that is funny (if you are funny and don't have that above) OR something that is totally different from 1, 2, 3, and 4.

If you have access to different sides of your voice (legit, belt, mix), make sure you have a variety of repertoire that showcases this.

> **Tip 16:** I would recommend having your cuts scanned and saved digitally to your phone, computer, or iPad so you have a backup copy if something happens to your book.
>
> **Tip 17:** Make sure nothing is in your book that you are not ready to sing, because, inevitably, that is what we will choose.

Where Do I Find Appropriate Material?

- Your Voice Teacher

Many students will get their repertoire from their voice teachers and many of those wonderful voice teachers come from an opera background. Whether they intend to or not, sometimes they want us to hear what they have done with your voice. But you know what? We want to hear your voice, not theirs. I have the upmost respect for voice teachers. Their job at your age is to make sure your voice is healthy and well aligned. Just make sure they are not having you sing anything that is out of your vocal reach and that you are singing your material in a stylistically appropriate way. For example, you would not belt "My White Night" from *The Music Man*, and you wouldn't riff in "Corner of the Sky" from *Pippin*.

- Your Vocal Coach, Drama Teacher, or Choir Teacher

A vocal coach is *"your own personal music director. They are first and foremost a collaborative pianist"* (Joel Waggoner). They are (usually) not a voice teacher because their focus is not about vocal technique. It is more about helping with repertoire, musical style, and the connection between the music and the lyric. Vocal coaches are often excellent pianists and will help you learn your music in the way that you will perform it. They also can record accompaniment tracks for you to rehearse with and to use when auditioning for Unifieds.

Your choir teacher or drama teacher should also be able to recommend songs or shows that would be great for you to research.

- Roles You Have Played

There is no reason for you not to sing from shows that you have done if they are age-appropriate. Think about it: you know the character, it is in your body and voice and you have already performed the material with nerves. If you loved the role and it is really right for you, this could be a good option. I wouldn't do this, however, if you played an older role or the song doesn't work well out of the context of the show. For example, if you played Herr Schultz in *Cabaret*, it would not be appropriate to sing "Married" from the show because that character is at least fifty years old, but if you played Nina in *In the Heights*, then why not use it?

- YouTube

Go to YouTube and look at the showcases from the schools you are applying to and see what kind of material they are singing. It will not only give you a sense of the program's style and "vibe," but it is a great way to trigger your research. Once you identify a song you like, look up the show and the writers. From there, make a list of other shows they wrote.

However, look out for the YouTube trap. I know that many, if not most, of you will listen to your songs on YouTube. This is a legitimate form of research and can be an excellent resource, but I have to warn you that you really should not learn your songs from YouTube. Many times the performances you watch will not reflect what is written in the music. You must learn your song from the sheet music. Trust me, we will know if you are singing a YouTube version: we know how the songs should go. Also, your accompanist probably didn't watch that video and will play what is in front of them. This isn't to say you can't make the song your own, but just make sure you are doing it after knowing what is on the page first.

- Online Websites

Good possibilities are Musicaltheatersongs.com, Musicnotes.com, and Sheetmusicdirect.com.

- Research on Your Own

Listen, listen, listen. Research, research, research. Pick a show a week and listen to the whole thing. Especially shows from the Golden Age that you have heard of but don't know.

Identify actors who have your essence or who are playing roles that you think you could play now. Look up other shows that they have done and find music that way.

Acting Your Song

Lyric and Song Analysis

All the songs you select must be *immediately actable*. By this I mean the lyric should take us on a journey and have an easily definable need or want. The song may relate to the character's journey within the context of the show, but many of these songs can stand alone, away from the show, and still present the emotions and needs of the character clearly. You may be surprised to know that many schools do not expect you to perform your audition song in the context of the show. They will, however, expect you to know what the context of the show is, as that is an important access into the song.

You are not expected to sing your song in the exact context of the show for your audition. This means that you can use the lyrics to create a new scenario for the song, keeping the same needs and wants of the character, but making them your own. How fun is that? In or out of context, you absolutely *must* know what you are singing about. You have to be the expert on the song and be able to answer all the questions I ask below in your sleep.

Think of "I'm Gonna Wash That Man" from *South Pacific*, for example. While Nellie is talking about a very specific moment in her life while performing a very specific task, we don't expect you to sing the song in a bikini with a towel in your hand, as the moment in the show is staged. We expect you to understand the context of the song within the show but not necessarily sing it that way for your audition. You can still show us that you are resolute in your decision to move on from a troubling situation (the want or objective of the song) without needing it to be within a scene from *South Pacific*. This is not an audition for the role of Nellie Forbush, and we want you to find your own way "into" the song while honoring the intention of the lyrics. In other words, you can create your own context for the song and not present it directly within the circumstances of the show. You are more than welcome to sing your material in the original context if you wish, but the reality is that you will be the only one who knows exactly what circumstances you are using.

> **Tip 18:** As well as understanding the context, know the writers of your song and show. You would be surprised how many applicants don't know who wrote their song or how to pronounce their names properly.

In every song you sing—just like your monologue—you must analyze the lyric so you are absolutely clear about what the song is saying. To do that, start by answering the following questions.

- Who Are You Singing To?

Most high school students I work with will almost always say that they are singing to themselves. This is not the strongest choice, as, ideally, you want to be singing *to* someone. Your song is a conversation with that person. It is often beneficial to pick the highest-stakes person you can think of and sing to them. The "highest-stakes person" means the person it would be hardest to sing these words to because of how it might affect them or you. Sometimes, the person you sing to can be a younger or older version of yourself. This can prove effective, as it is still a conversation and not just an inner monologue in song form. Try it and see if it works for you.

- What Is Your Objective?

Another way to ask this is—What do you want? What are you asking for? What do you want your scene partner to understand? There is always a reason for a song in musical theater: often because a character has a need and doesn't know how to fulfill it. Figure out what you need in your song and use that information to guide you.

- What Is Your Obstacle?

What is in the way of getting what you want? Are you singing to your mom because she won't let you go to prom? Are you just now realizing that you deserve to be happy despite the fact that your brother died? Do you long for a different life but are trapped in the one you have? Defining your obstacle can help you figure out what you need to overcome to reach your objective.

- What Are Your Tactics?

What are you going to do to get what you want? I often think that you can play three tactics in a 32-bar cut (or one minute) and really just one or two in a 16-bar cut. Tactics are usually active verbs. If you are trying to make your lover stay, you could—*make* her laugh, then *beg* her to listen, and when all else fails, *plead* for forgiveness. Each tactic is part of the journey, the steps you take to reach your objective, and often will build in intensity.

- What Is at Stake?

What do you have to lose? If you don't say these words, will you regret it forever? Are you so happy that you don't want to let the moment go? Is the love you feel so powerful that you have to tell him before it is too late? The "stakes" are the reasons you are singing in the first place. When someone tells you to "raise the stakes," they are asking you to have a better reason for singing this song, to have more to lose. Watching someone put herself out there bravely and honestly is exciting.

- Why Do You Have to Sing This Song Right Now?

What makes this moment important and urgent? Is the bus about to leave? Is your lover about to walk out the door? Is the prom tomorrow night? If you don't say what you need to, will your heart burst?

- Where Are You?

What do you see? What do you smell? Are you in a familiar place or not? Is it public and crowded, or quiet and intimate? Does the place bring back memories or make you feel afraid? We behave differently depending on the location.

Once you have picked material you love, can sing well, and have rehearsed a million different ways, you should feel like you *own* this material. It will not matter at all if the person ahead of you sang the same song, because no one will possibly do it like you.

Here is a great story from Professor Robert Meffe, Department Head of the MFA Musical Theater Program at San Diego State University, about hearing the same song at an audition:

"One day I was playing auditions for Sweeney Todd, *and a gentleman came in with the song "Funny" from* City of Angels. *He sang, he was rather mediocre, and they weren't interested in casting him. But as soon as he left the room, everyone behind the table started railing on what a poor audition choice "Funny" was for this call. It's all they could talk about, even to the point of wondering if they should tell the casting director to get word to the actor that he shouldn't use that song at an audition. Fast forward to later that same day, and a friend of mine comes in to audition for the title role of Sweeney. Lo and behold he plops down "Funny" in front of me as his audition song. I am torn; do I tell him that the table actively hates this song? Do I subtly suggest he find a different song? I choose the path of least resistance, knowing that an actor prepares for an audition*

and they should put their best foot forward. So I sit down and play. And he's really good. I mean, really good. The table all sit up in rapt attention and hang on every word. They are wildly enthusiastic after he is finished and they start talking about availability for this production. They end up casting him as Sweeney Todd from this audition. All well and good for my friend, but the moral of this story comes from one observation: not one person behind the table remarked that this was the same song that they heard just a few hours ago and despised. If the first actor could have gotten feedback on his audition, he would have received this, "Don't ever do that song. It's a terrible audition song." When in reality, it was probably just not a very good audition, and he was not right for the role of Sweeney. What I have always taken from this story is that it is not as important WHAT you sing, but HOW you sing it."

I want to encourage you to live in the lyrics of the song and be emotionally and physically connected. I encourage you to use the space in a thoughtful way, to make bold choices and truly BRING IT. If there was ever a time to lay it all down, it is now. "Do not throw away your shot." ☺

Tip 19: Start with your best song first and if you can't decide what is best, then start with the up tempo. We love a good up tempo because it is typically high energy and is usually a great way to introduce you to the audition panel. Think of it this way: you want to start with your strongest piece first because you never know what might happen in the room. You could get cut off for some reason, or we may decide after your first song that we want to hear another option instead of what you planned to sing second.

Tip 20: Some schools will say that they don't want to hear songs that are currently on Broadway, but some won't mind at all. In fact, if you sing a song from a role in a show that you could play now, then it tells us that you have a clear idea of what roles you might play in the future. Just make sure that you are truly ready to tackle that material. If you can't sing "The Wizard and I" from *Wicked*, but you like the song and you think you could play Elphaba one day—then please do not sing it for your audition. It is a big song for an advanced singer. If you are there and can totally nail it, then there is nothing more exciting than hearing a flawless rendition of "The Wizard and I."

Tip 21: If you play an instrument expertly and you know there is a role you could play that requires that instrument, it might not hurt to prepare a song from that show on your instrument, in addition to the songs that are already being asked of you. For example, if you play the piano (again expertly), and you sing the material from the musical *Beautiful*, then offering one of those songs as an option could be an additional supplement. Or, if you are perfect for the lead role in *Once* and you play the guitar, consider preparing a song from that show and offering it as an option. The conversation in the room would go like this: "I have 'X song' from 'Y Show,' but I also have 'X song' with my guitar if that would interest you at all. What would you prefer?"

What If Everything about the Songs Fits Perfectly Except the Key?

Andrew Byrne, one of New York City's premier voice teachers has this to say about the key of your song: *"The composer of your song selected an original key for the piece, but you should ask yourself if the song is in the right key for you. Sheet music is available and transposable online, so if you love the piece but it doesn't feel like it's sitting right in your voice, transposition may be a good option. Many times, even a half-step up or down can make all the difference in the world. However, there are some iconic songs where the original key is expected; we use these well-known pieces as an assessment of your vocal skills. For instance, if you sing 'The Story Goes On' from* Baby, *we expect you to sing it in C major so we can hear how you handle the ending."*

Tip 22: Listen to your song's accompaniment without any singing and investigate what it is telling you musically and dramatically. You will be amazed at what it can teach you about the song.

Chapter Takeaway

New Song, Same You

This chapter is FULL of information. So much so, that it might take a few readings to understand and apply all of the techniques and suggestions. I would recommend rereading each section as you come to it in your song journey—obsessing about how to act your song when you still are choosing what to sing will not be helpful. Let's break down each step below, as a reminder.

- List each school's song requirements (they will often overlap), so you know what song types you need. Writing this out will help you not overlook any outlying requests.
- Ask for recommendations from anyone and everyone who knows you and your talent.
  - You don't have to sing anything suggested, but they might open your eyes to a gem of a show you never knew, with another song that fits you to a tee.
- Make a list of every song you, and your immediate circle, can think of that fits the requirements and may be a good fit. Anything.
- Once you have your list, look for reasons the song may not work for an audition.
  - Go back to the sections "Choosing Your Songs" and "Song Types" for help narrowing this list down.
  - Don't forget that the song has to be right for YOU, no matter how great or popular the song is.
  - Be a bit ruthless; that list was every possible song, but you want to make your decision easier in the end.
- Pick your songs!
  - Don't toss the other songs that made it this far! They could be very good songs to fill out your book.
- Make your cuts based on the requirements of each school (see the cutting tips above and in chapter 9).
  - Start with the smallest time or bar allowances—you can always sing more of the song or another song, but going over the requirements will not look good.
  - If this is very difficult, you may need to choose another song (good thing you still have that list now, right?).
- If you need tracks, make sure that you record them as soon as you can!
  - This could be another way to practice at home too.
- Now go back to the full song—and the show itself—to figure out your context and your acting objectives.
  - Refer to the "Acting Your Song" section, and even write out the answers to the questions for each song and character.
- And, of course, practice makes better. Get to it!

5 | "Say It Somehow"
MONOLOGUES

WITH GRANT KRETCHIK

We're happy to hear two contrasting monologues. The term "contrast" is pretty broad and allows students to show what they do well. Often, young actors don't have a lot of experience, understanding, or passion for verse drama, so, unless they do it well, I would rather not see it. Again, my constant refrain is, do what you do well. The audition is not only an assessment of how developed your talent is at this point, it is also your introduction to us. We want to meet you through your audition pieces and what you do with them. So, requiring something you don't do well doesn't serve either of us.

— Joe Deer, Chair, Department of Theatre, Dance, and Motion Pictures, and Director of the Musical Theatre Initiative, Wright State University

ANOTHER COMPONENT OF YOUR AUDITION will be the monologue. Programs will most often ask for two contrasting pieces—just as they ask for two contrasting songs—as a way for you to demonstrate different skill sets and ultimately show your range. While it is safe to assume contrasting means classical and contemporary, that distinction alone is not the only way to show your range and ability. Regardless, it is important that you *read with care* what each school is requiring; as an auditor, there is nothing more disappointing then realizing the person in front of you has not taken the time to read the requirements.

> **Tip 1:** As you can see, we stress over and over in this book to read the requirements for every audition you plan on attending. Each school is slightly different in what they are looking for, and tailoring your material to meet those specific desires can go a long way. Don't worry: we will keep reminding you throughout the rest of the book.

Let's explore some key words relating to Monologues:

- Contrasting

This means presenting material that is contrasting in style (i.e., classical vs. contemporary), regardless of whether it is comedic or dramatic, which helps show your ability to handle different styles. I would encourage you to think about how YOU can demonstrate range and not simply allow the contrast in style do the work for you. Avoid portraying a charter who, regardless of the style or period of the work, is experiencing the same circumstances, needs, and emotions in both pieces.

- A *classical* piece is considered to be from a play prior to 1900. It is important to understand that this typically means we want to hear your facility for language. A classical text presents its own set of demands, and we are interested in your skill or even your intuition toward language, rhythm, and dynamics.
- *Contemporary* is defined as material from the twentieth and twenty-first centuries, so, in its basic sense, anything after 1900. However, there is a lot of material from both categories that fall on either side of 1900, and I would not use these definitions as an absolute guide to contrasting material. For example, Ibsen and Chekov are pre-1900 (authors considered classical) and in many ways have similar language demands to Tennessee Williams or Arthur Miller (both considered contemporary by definition). In selecting your contemporary monologue, I would look at plays that are written in everyday speech.

- Verse and Heightened Language

Drama was considered a subgenre of poetry for a long time. This matters because poetry aims to express ideas in a form that is more expressive than everyday language; it's more complex or elevated, and is considered heightened language. Classical plays written during this time were written with the rules of poetry in mind, and they are often in verse with heightened language.

- Comedy

What makes something funny? Everyone will have a different answer to this question. I find comedic monologues and comedy in general work best when the content is a little bit wrong to say but also has a little truth to it. I tell my students that comedy isn't funny to the people it's happening to. But finding a truly comedic monologue can be difficult and performing it can be even harder. We want to see that you understand the jokes and can still bring an element of honesty to it. But we will also want to see that you understand the rhythm of comedy too, the setting up and landing of a joke.

- ## Drama

An important distinction must be made between drama and theatricality. Theatricality is the style or aesthetic of how material is presented, and I find this will not serve you in these types of auditions. Drama, on the other hand, is what exists between two characters. A dramatic monologue has a tendency to take on more serious issues and is filled with emotion. However, it is very important that in your dramatic monologue you are careful not to "play the emotion." Emotions are the result of pursuing an objective and failing or succeeding to achieve it.

> **Tip 2:** Regardless of how many songs you sing or monologues you are asked to prepare and subsequently perform in the room, avoid thinking that your monologues and songs are independent of each other. In other words, prepare the whole package. You can demonstrate your range by selecting monologues that contrast with your song selection in addition to two contrasting songs. All your material choices will be recorded on your audition forms, and the auditors will be able to see how well rounded and thoughtful your choices were.

Amy here! Many students wonder if contrasting always means to prepare a classical and a contemporary monologue. As is often the case, there is no one answer; every school has different requirements. It is always best to check the program's website and add the guidelines to your chart so you can see if you even need a classical monologue or if two contrasting contemporary pieces will do.

But I wanted to give you a little insight from a few colleagues as to why a program would ask for a classical piece and also why not. This can hopefully help you make a decision on the material you use, depending on your skill set:

We do ask for a classical piece. We are a conservatory program for acting/ Musical Theater training, and it is important for us to see how a student

handles the challenge of speaking heightened language and finding the
means to incorporating it truthfully into a performance.

—Barbara MacKenzie-Wood, Raymond W. Smith Professor of Acting,

Carnegie Mellon University, School of Drama

We ask for two contrasting one-minute monologues. Many applicants are
asked to prepare classical pieces [for other programs], so they choose to
do one as part of our audition. We are happy to see classical pieces, but it's
best for us to see contemporary or modern work, since working with clas-
sical text is part of our training. We have no expectations that they should
have mastered the complexities of that by their senior year in high school.

—Catherine Weidner, Chair, Department of Theatre Arts, Ithaca College

We don't ask for a classical monologue. Our auditions at Penn State usually
only include one monologue—and we like to hear something more natural,
age-appropriate, and contemporary. Classical work is part of our training,
but it's much easier to get a read on a young artist in something more natu-
ralistic when we only have a minute to listen to speech and acting choices.

—John Simpkins, Head of Musical Theatre, Penn State University

Choosing Your Monologues

Just like your songs, choosing a monologue can be hard. Perhaps because
a monologue won't only demonstrate that you can act, which isn't always
as relevant as you might think especially once you've established that you
indeed can. But a monologue can tell us much more about who you are,
your personality, your intellect, your sense of humor, if you read plays or
not, and what types of plays you are drawn to. There is or there should
be something deeply personal about selecting your material, and subse-
quently that can be somewhat personally revealing.

Things to Consider When Looking for Effective Material

- Age Range

Select something in your *natural age range* or with circumstances that are
understandable to you. I would also recommend keeping your choices to
monologues that are about human relationships and conflict rather than
overarching political or moral messages. As such, you might want to avoid

overly political playwrights such as Athol Fugard and Bertolt Brecht. This, of course, isn't an absolute.

- Length

Keep it short, at 60 seconds or 90 seconds at the most. Once again, look at the requirements of each school and follow them. Presenting a monologue that is 2–3 minutes long says to the auditors you didn't care enough to prepare properly.

- Identification with Your Monologue

Do you *love it* and does it *entertain* you? It is important that you identify with your monologue and can relate to or at a minimum understand the circumstances of the character.

- Context

Sometimes we can fall in love with a play or a scene, but that doesn't mean the corresponding monologue will stand on its own. Does the monologue have enough action and compelling conflict when it is not presented in the context of the play? Does the character want something in this specific moment? Is the material entertaining? Or is the monologue reporting exposition or explaining some other event in the play or the world of the character? The latter might be an indication that the monologue isn't great on its own.

- Playing to Your Type

While it is important to perform monologues that you love, it is equally important to pick something that suits you as an actor. If you don't know your "type," ask your teachers and directors how they would cast you. Or ask yourself what roles you might be cast in on film and TV. We might all want to be Jake Gyllenhaal or Halle Berry, but some of us are Seth Rogen or Kathy Bates. Which is great! We need all types of actors in Musical Theater and we want your monologue choices to reflect that you know who you are.

- Playing to Your Strengths

Can you cry easily? Go for the dramatic scene full of loss. If not, then prepare a monologue with more tension and less emotion and avoid saying, "I'm crying." Are you funny? Do people other than your family and friends laugh when you tell a story? Go for big comedy. But if you can't land a joke, then maybe a "seriocomic" monologue where you can pursue objectives playfully is the way to go. Are you fantastic at reciting poetry or the rhythm of verse? Choose a classical piece that is written in prose.

- Strong Characters

It is too easy and boring for an actor to be a victim of circumstance. It is much more compelling to watch someone trying to survive. It's not about your character winning or losing—that is up to the playwright—it's the struggle to get what you want or die trying. We are moved when we watch someone fighting through emotions or trying to rise out of their own despair. Earn the right to shed a tear or raise your voice with your determination to get through the material's presented circumstances.

What to Avoid

- Narrowing Your Choices

Are you performing monologues only from plays that might be on your high school reading list for your literature or English classes? Such titles would be *Our Town, Death of a Salesman, Who's Afraid of Virginia Woolf?, A Raisin in the Sun, The Glass Menagerie,* and so on. These are wonderful plays, and a great audition with a monologue from one of them is still a great audition. But you want your choices to reflect you and your interests. Read new plays. Seek out exciting new material. Research everywhere— online, your school and public library, ask friends and mentors. Take the time to find something that you can connect to and that really shows you off.

- Dialects

We want to hear your natural voice, and when you "put on" a dialect you create an added barrier for us. There is material that really demands a particular dialect or cadence, and it's good material, but it might be best for you to avoid it unless you have a natural disposition to that sound.

Take Tennessee Williams, for example. His characters and language almost require an iconic southern sound and cadence. And while I love his writing, I am auditioning YOU, not the monologue itself. If you come in with Williams and you don't have the dialect mastered, the material isn't nearly as rich and can land slightly flat. If you try to "put on" the dialect, then we have the issue of not hearing your authentic voice. If you *are* predisposed to a southern dialect and choose to perform Williams, I recommend that you pair it with another piece that is told in your natural voice.

- Heightened Language

Shakespeare's works performed with a British dialect would be considered *heightened language.* There is a false idea out there that using a British dialect is required for your classical monologue. Or that a "Mid-Atlantic" dialect is necessary for Shakespeare because you've watched American classical actors utilize it in some productions. This is not necessary for your audition. Performing Shakespeare in your natural speaking voice is quite common, and it allows us to hear you over the dialect you are trying to perfect. Instead, look to really dig deep into the text and the meter to understand the piece as a whole. The *Shakespeare Lexicon and Quotation Dictionary* by Alexander Schmidt is a great reference tool.

- Sonnets

While some people don't mind you performing a sonnet for your classical monologue, I do not recommend it. Sonnets are poems that can be used to introduce acting students to iambic pentameter. They are not monologues, though, because they lack momentum, action, and character motives.

Take Sonnet 18, "Shall I Compare Thee to a Summer's Day?" It is a beautiful poem that is thought to have many similarities to Romeo's balcony speech from Act II, Scene 2, of *Romeo and Juliet.* The difference for the actor in these speeches is that Sonnet 18 is a full recitation of love, whereas Romeo's speech is a declaration of love against the odds stacked against him. Romeo's speech possesses the dramatic elements that make acting so exciting: he is emotionally full, he has to overcome his emotions to speak to Juliet, there is danger in his confession, and he could be killed if he is found in the garden by his enemy. Romeo's speech takes the actor on a journey through love from discovery to confession; it is active in a way that Sonnet 18 is not.

- Experimental Nonlinear Work

Nonlinear, metaphorical, and experimental work presents challenges in the audition room. If you select a monologue that is hard for us to follow when taken out of context, we spend our energy trying to understand the work and lose sight of you and how you approached the text. This writing is often open to broad interpretations that make it harder for us to assess your choices and your capacity for truth and honesty in your work. An actor can easily get stuck playing ideas, metaphors, and moody obscurity rather than honest, "actable" objectives. Luisa's monologue from *The Fantasticks* (perhaps considered fantasy), where she is described as brushing her hair as it changes colors, is filled with broad metaphors and descriptions of fantasy. It is difficult to act and harder still for us to see your choices. Excellent writers who often do not make the most successful monologues in the audition room are Thornton Wilder, Samuel Beckett, Jean Genet, and Eugene Ionesco.

- Disabled or Sociopathic Characters

While I believe everyone's story needs to be told, there are many reasons you want to avoid this during an audition. In regards to disabled characters, you must perform this with such integrity and skill that it truly demonstrates your abilities. Otherwise it could likely come off as a stereotype and offend your auditor. As for sociopathic characters, while you might play this type of character well, you want to avoid us feeling scared or creeped out by you. In either case, these types of characters can keep the "youness" that is you from shining through. You have to imagine part of this audition involves us deciding if we are excited and comfortable spending the next four years together.

- Monologues from Musicals

While there are some worthy monologues in Musical Theater librettos, typically, spoken text in a musical isn't as complex because the best Musical Theater monologues become songs. For example, *A Chorus Line* has some good monologues but they are mostly exposition for the song that follows.

> **Tip 3:** I strongly recommend avoiding stand-alone monologues, or those monologues that are not from published plays or films. (Be careful with film monologues; not every school appreciates a monologue from a film or TV show. Check the requirements and call the program if you are unsure.)

Tip 4: Go to the back cover of the script and read the summary. Ask yourself, "Is this something I connect to? Is there a part in here for me?" Then find the character breakdown in the script or online and ask yourself, "Am I right for any of these parts?" If yes, then read the play; there might be something in it for you. If no, still consider reading the play at a later date. Many actors do not read enough.

Overall, I would suggest applicants choose material from plays and musicals that you love, characters that connect to you, and a role that you could play right now. Avoid sexually charged language or situations; this is not the time for that. Practice the changes in the piece, when is there a beat or a shift that forces you to make a new choice, play a tactic, or work off an imaginary response from another character? Be sure to do a few mock auditions, and include your introduction in that practice.

—Catherine Weidner, Chair, Department of Theatre Arts, Ithaca College

Preparing the Monologue

When selecting a monologue, we often approach the search with a specific end goal in mind, such as "will it let me show emotion *x*?" Under the pressure of finding "the perfect monologue," we forget its true merit: a monologue is an important moment for a character to express her feelings in a way that is so significant, she refuses to stop talking, or allow others to interrupt her, until she has fully expressed the vitality of the moment. A monologue is a little story filled with the epic struggles and/or triumphs of the larger story of the play. We actors are storytellers who interpret the written word of the playwright and also the emotional and psychological journey of the character. However, when we search for a monologue for an audition, we rarely look at the whole story. We approach it from the point of view of the end result: will this monologue show that I can cry, be intense, angry, funny, flirtatious, dominating, submissive? This goal restricts the actor's ability to play the true and full complexity of what the character may want, or think, or feel. It can lead to a one-dimensional idea of what these characters might be experiencing.

Once you find a monologue that serves you, it's time to prepare for your audition. It is important you take your time and dig into the monologue, the play, and the character. Jumping to the end result of what you hope the monologue demonstrates about your abilities will only leave gaping holes in your work. I often say to my students, "You are decorating the Christmas tree but you have failed to even buy the tree."

How to Prepare Your Monologue

- Read the Script

Read it, and then read the script again. Your mind, body, and voice are vehicles for the thoughts and actions of the character, and you *must* understand the sequence of events that have led to the moment of the monologue. Additionally, the script is filled with both truth and lies, and if you fail to read the script, you will fail to understand the character's point of view on all things related to her world, such as other characters, events, politics, and so on. Also, if the auditor asks about the play, you'll be prepared to discuss it.

- Ask Questions

You first want to start asking questions such as, what is the play trying to say or teach? What are the themes of the play? How do the characters contribute to the theme? It is important to know the world of the play and these questions can help fulfill some of the storytelling obligations not immediately presented in the monologue. Additionally, the audition committee might ask you questions about the play and you will want to demonstrate that you not only read it, but also understand it.

- Ask Questions about the Character

What does the character want? How does she think and feel about her circumstances in the play? Does the character fail or succeed? How does the monologue fit into the character's journey? What is your character's objective in the monologue? Is he trying to convince someone of something or to motivate someone into action? Understand what your character's goals are throughout the play as well as within the specific moment of the monologue.

- Define the Character's Objective

What does the character want, or what is the character's ultimate goal? Remember you want to WIN or die trying to win. It is important that you define this goal in a way that is alive and active. Actors often overly complicate objectives. We tend to summarize the complications of the drama within the circumstances. When I ask a student what do you want?, I often get a response such as "I want this guy to ask me out on a date because I like him. But I can't because he's dating my best friend and my best friend is just getting over the death of her dog. So I guess what I want is to just hang out with both of them." No! Never! Do not make excuses for your character's wants and desires! Let's try again, what do you want? "I want to go on a date with this guy." Why? "So I can make him my boyfriend!" YES! Yes, you do! The point is that defining an objective is often easier then we make it. Keep it simple, active, and very important to you. This is where you hear the phrase "life or death," which simply means raise the stakes, win or die trying.

- Define the Consequences of Not Getting What You Want

In our example, "I want this guy to ask me out. If he doesn't, he won't become my boyfriend and then I won't have a date to the prom, or, worse, I could die alone." Suddenly the objective becomes really important. Objectives often have to do with needing, love, friendship, sex, protection, revenge, or escape, something your character is missing that needs to be satisfied in some way. And not fulfilling those needs would be unbearable for the character. She must win.

- Beats

In a monologue, a beat is a discovery that causes the character to adjust how he will achieve his objective. To understand beats, ask yourself, what is different about the character at the end of the monologue? Has he succeeded or failed? These changes form the arch of the monologue, and the beats define the actions or tactics used to achieve (or not) the character's objective. An action is what the character says or does to WIN his objective, and the action is the verb you attach to each beat. In the example above, where the objective is to go on a date, the different beats or tactics or actions of the monologue might be defined as to seduce, to persuade, to flatter. When you switch between tactics, you take a beat.

- Behavior

How does your comprehension of the character's circumstances and objectives connect to your body, breath, and voice? How can we express these feelings physically in a truthful moment? Discovering how these actions and tactics live in your body is the most important part of the monologue process. If your action is to flirt, imagine what your body, face, breath, and voice are doing as you flirt to get what you want. Explore how your posture changes, how you hold your head, where you focus your eyes, the speed of your breath. Then move to your next tactic and see how that action changes you physically. To confess is very different than to challenge, which is very different from to dismiss, and each will inhabit your body differently too.

> **Tip 5:** Actions, tactics, and behaviors are always used to achieve the character's objectives, but they are not always successful. The character must try flirting first, because that is what she does best, and only when it fails, does she try confessing her love. As the actor, you know the flirting will fail, but you must let the character try anyway. You have "actor knowledge" of what will ultimately happen, but the character doesn't know the end, and will try many different tactics to achieve her objective. Let her.

- Who Are You Talking To?

There is always someone listening to your monologue, thereby making it a dialogue, and it is important to know who that person is. But a more important question is, *what are they doing* while you are talking? The person on the receiving end will be directly connected to your objective and the actions you pick to achieve that objective. But what do they want from YOU? This can help you establish what they are doing, how they are reacting to your speech, and how you will deal with it. Their behavior while "listening" will affect the tactics and behaviors you choose to get what you want from them.

> **Tip 6:** Turn your monologue into a dialogue. Write it out. Ask yourself the following questions about what your monologue "partner" is doing. When do they agree or disagree with what I am saying? Do they take a breath as if to speak and interrupt me? Do they want to calm me down? Are they getting up to leave? Do they attempt to come closer to me? These decisions about how they are behaving in response to what you are saying and doing will cause you to "deal with them" differently, or to change your tactics.

For example, If I am talking and I observe someone rolling their eyes in disagreement, that will change how I attempt to convince them that I am right. If I fail and they start to pack up their backpack and stand up to leave, I will adjust to that. It will become more important that I raise my voice and call after them in an effort to stop them. If it helps, write out what the listener is doing and ask someone you trust to play that part as you rehearse. Once you feel comfortable with your behavior changes in response to the other person, continue practicing alone.

- Define Where You Are

The environment and sense of place are very impactful and can change the stakes for your character. For example, if you are going "to confront" a lover who has cheated, this type of monologue can change based on where it takes place. In your bedroom, you have permission to be vocally and physically strong in your tactics; you two are alone. However, in a crowded café, your objective will still be to confront, but having thirty other people sitting around you will change your tactics. Now there is a risk of embarrassment by being overheard. You may be more careful in choosing your words and their volume.

Three Things We Love to See in the Monologue Audition

Amy again! If the monologue is a stressful part of the process for you, here is some advice from my colleagues around the country as to what they love to see in auditions. This is really great info that you can incorporate into your practice and performance.

- *A strong objective*
- *Fearless pursuit of actions that are designed to achieve that objective— with voice, text, and full body commitment*
- *A connection to the person to whom they are speaking, and the courage to listen to that person even within the shape of a monologue. This ability to listen tells me volumes about the kind of actor they have the capability of being.*

—John Simpkins, Head of Musical Theatre, Penn State University

- *We love to watch actors who can think.*
- *We appreciate when the monologue has something spontaneous about it—when the actor is open to making a new choice or having a new idea in the audition room.*
- *We love it when the material is well written and the actor can relate to it.*

—Tracey Moore, Professor, The Hartt School, Theatre Division,
University of Hartford

- *Age-appropriate, intelligent material. Your choice of monologue (much like the song selection) tells me a lot about you as an artist.*
- *A truthful and articulate emotional inner life. Connected moment-to-moment work will speak for itself.*
- *Clear focus and stillness. This tells me that the actor trusts himself/herself and the material.*

—Hank Stratton, Assistant Professor, Acting/Musical Theater Division,
University of Arizona

- *Believability.*
- *A clear understanding of the material from a thematic basis, illustrating that you really know what you are talking about. Be familiar with the content of the monologue: what is the writer saying?*
- *That the actor has an emotional connection to the material. Doesn't mean an actor has to "show" emotion but has to be able to access an appropriate emotional connection that informs the material.*

—Kaitlin Hopkins, Head of Musical Theatre, Texas State University

- *A natural delivery with obvious connection to a scene partner.*
- *Material that shows us a real person; a character that is similar to the actual personality of the actor in front of us.*
- *No excessive swearing, yelling, or talk about sex, rape, dead people/animals.*

—Matt Edwards, Associate Professor and Coordinator of Musical Theatre Voice,
Shenandoah University

- *Establishing a clear connection to the material and a relationship to the other (if applicable).*
- *Physical and vocal groundedness; being present in their body.*

- *Making choices with regard to beat changes, given circumstances, and stakes, reflected in moment-to-moment work.*

> —Catherine Weidner, Chair, Department of Theatre Arts, Ithaca College

- *Honesty (talking to another person).*
- *Focus (focusing on another person).*
- *Humor (positive approach to the material).*

> —Mark Madama, Associate Professor of Musical Theatre,
> University of Michigan

- *An actor who is connected (emotionally, physically, and vocally) to the material and who can communicate the material with truth and spontaneity.*
- *An actor who is brave, open and not afraid to take risks and use themselves.*
- *An actor who is bright, intelligent, and open in the interview portion of the audition.*

> —Barbara MacKenzie-Wood, Raymond W. Smith Professor
> of Acting, Carnegie Mellon University, School of Drama

Chapter Takeaway

A Go-to Guide for the Monologue Audition Room

DO

- Be polite to EVERYONE. This includes the person checking you in and the person monitoring the door. We talk to each other.
- Slate. Avoid asking, "Should I slate?" YES! Just slate. Preparing your slate is a part of preparing your audition. If you wait until the last minute to practice this, your nerves may get in the way. A simple "Hi, my name is _____ and this is a monologue from _____ by _____" works great.
- Walk in with confidence and poise. We know you are nervous but remember we are truly rooting for you. We need you to be the right fit for us as much as you want to be the right fit.
- You can smile and say hello and goodbye. Don't let your nervousness keep you from being warm and friendly.
- Do have a point of focus on the wall. It is best to focus just above the heads of the auditors, or just to the left or right of them. When I say just, I mean just.
- Know who wrote the play and how to pronounce their name. I have heard it all: Neil Laboot, Thornton Wilder wrote *The Importance of Being Earnest*, and even that Samuel French wrote *A Feminine Ending*. This play is by Sarah Treem, and Samuel French is the publishing company who holds the rights to license this, and many other plays. Examples like this make you stand out for all the wrong reasons.
- Do read the whole play. We may ask you about the play and its circumstances, and if it is immediately clear that you failed to read and understand it, this can affect our decision. We love what we do and we endeavor to do it with intelligence and integrity. We want to work with others who will do the same.

DON'T

- Chairs! Chairs! Chairs! If there is a chair there, use it, no need to ask. If there is not one, then by all means ask; it is your audition. But DO NOT use a chair to face you as your scene partner. It is unnecessary and pulls your focus down during your monologue. Also, if you sit for one piece, stand for the other. We want to see your behavior and physicality throughout your monologues, and a chair can cut you off from your body. A move from sitting to standing, or the reverse, can convey a change in emotion, but often it can just be distracting. Really, JUST DON'T USE A CHAIR.

- Don't play your monologue to one of the auditors.
- Don't go over the time allowed. It comes across as selfish and shows us that you don't follow instructions. Also don't linger in the room. Even if you are cut off, say thank you when your time is up and head for the door. You don't want to wear out your welcome.

- Do not show us your preparation in the room. I have witnessed too many young actors who have been terribly misled, or have some false perceptions of "taking a moment" before starting a monologue. In my experience, and conversations with colleagues, young actors who take advantage or abuse the concept of "taking a moment" leave us with an impression that the actor is overly precious about their process and might present challenges in future training. While I personally don't care to see an actor put their head down for even a moment before beginning, I think it is fair to assume that is the most you can get away with. It may also be acceptable to briefly turn away and then turn back to step into the monologue, but in either case the key word here is brief. This "moment" should be no more than 5 seconds. That's it. Otherwise, consider slating your name and monologue, and just going right into it with only a beat. Either way while standing before the committee, avoid the following:
  - Dropping your head for too long before speaking
  - Gazing up to the ceiling for too long
  - Using deep, heavy breaths that we can see and hear
  - Stretching or warming up while we wait for you to start

6 | "Putting It Together"
IT'S ALL IN THE DETAILS

WITH WAYNE PETRO

Know that we love young actors and are committed to helping you live your dreams. That begins at the audition and, for my school, from the moment you make email contact with us to find out about the programs. We audition a lot of people, but we want to treat all of you with dignity and respect.
—Joe Deer, Chair, Department of Theatre, Dance, and Motion Pictures, and
Director of the Musical Theatre Initiative, Wright State University

The Academic Application

Just as every college's audition process is a little different, so is the process for actually *getting in*, academically, to your prospective universities. The manner in which colleges link the academic application to the audition can vary widely, and you must remember that you will need to focus on this aspect just as much as your audition. Academics do matter!

Applying as a Freshman

- Deadlines

The first step in a successful audition is meeting the application deadlines and submitting all materials on time. All deadlines will be published on the school's website, but if you find them hard to locate, just call the admission counselor. Most universities offer a few different deadlines as well: early decision, early action, priority, or regular admittance. Schools that offer early decision usually require a contract that binds you to accept if admitted. While this is rare for performing arts programs, because the audition usually happens after the academic decision, you *will* encounter it. For example, Pace University just started accepting applications for early decision. This will only apply to the few students who audition before the November 1 deadline, but it is still an option. One perk is that you will learn of your audition decision earlier too.

- Completing the Application

Most typically, a prospective student will have to file an application to the institution *before* beginning the audition process. How "complete" the application needs to be, however, will vary from school to school. Some college programs require the application to be fully complete— that is, you've submitted all standardized test-score reports, high school transcripts, letters of recommendation, essays, and any other materials the school requires. Other programs will allow you to proceed with the audition process while the application is incomplete. *Always check* the institution's policy on this (the first of many times I'll say this!). For many programs, a common mistake is waiting until you've been admitted to the university before starting the audition process. At institutions like Pace, the academic decision will arrive before the audition decision, but maybe not before the audition date.

- Varying Application Components

A quick web search of top Musical Theater programs reveals that not all institutions require SAT or ACT scores. Some want the essay submitted with the application and some want it uploaded online. The amount and method of receipt for the letters of recommendations are also different from school to school. The moral of the story is that colleges will make it *very clear* what they want in the application because we know how different we all are! Read each website carefully!

- Academic Admittance to the University

At Pace, a student is admitted for academic study as an undecided major until the result of her audition is known to admissions and to the student. If admitted, the undecided major changes to the proper program major within the School of Performing Arts. For those not admitted to the performing programs, the major remains undecided and the student may still attend the university. This is not the case, however, with all institutions.

At the other end of the spectrum are the institutions where the application to the college is also the application to the Musical Theater program.

The acceptance to the degree program and the college are one and the same. These are typically *conservatory-style programs* but can also exist at larger institutions where you apply directly to the arts college instead of through a general admission office.

I'm often asked the question, *"What options do I have if I'm not academically accepted to your school? Does my audition have any weight in the matter?"* Again, it depends on the institution. Generally speaking, however, if a school has an academic application requirement on top of, or separate from, the audition, a denial to the university means the process is over. But again, all schools have slightly different admissions parameters and rubrics, so a denial at one college does not mean it will be a denial at the rest. In *rare instances*, a highly successful audition might intercept a potential denial, or even rarer, cause a reversal, but I have only seen a couple of these scenarios play out. Students should *never* count on this happening and should *never* request a reversal of academic admission unless there is new information, such as an improved SAT or ACT score.

Applying as a Transfer Student

Colleges around the country are making it easier everyday for transfer students to apply to their institutions. At Pace, we even have "Transfer Tuesdays," where the application fee is waived and the prospective student can get their admission decision on the spot. I am sure other schools have these kinds of events, so if you are not happy with your current program or looking to apply into a performing arts program from an academic one at the same college, some of the steps above will apply, but not all. Here are a few helpful hints for the prospective transfer student.

- University Requirements

Presenting a high school transcript, SAT or ACT score reports, or other precollege materials will depend on how much college-level work is on your current college transcript. Keep in mind, however, that every university has its own policy regarding the acceptance of similar credits from another school. To give a prospective student an idea of some of the course equivalencies, Pace has a "Transfer Credit Equivalency" look-up online. Just note that this is only *some* of the course equivalencies that previous students have brought in, and it is in no way a comprehensive list.

- Transferring to a Performing Arts Program

This is slightly more complex. At auditions, I always tell the prospective transfer students in the room that each situation is completely unique. Determining factors to the final decision will include where you are transferring from and how long you were in that program, as well as your grades and the types of courses you took. The auditioning faculty will certainly not know all of this information in the room, but if you are being considered for admission, then this information becomes incredibly important. So important, in fact, that sometimes the decision and audition results will be delayed. The reasoning for this usually stems from the question, "Will this student join the first-year class or the second-year class?" At Pace, we only admit students in the fall terms, so we have to know if there will be space in the continuing student's class before admitting someone as a second-year.

Note: Some schools will *audition and admit students mid-year, but be sure to check with each program to see how that affects your ability to* truly *join that year's cohort.*

- First-Year Requirements

Transferring programs can sometimes be very tricky. At Pace, in addition to our very unique programs, we have many "traditional" programs with unique first-year requirements. As such, transfer students are *rarely admitted directly into the second-year class*—instead, they become part-first-year, part-second-year students. In this case, the transferring academic credits become even more important. If a student can transfer in a significant number of academic-based courses, we can sometimes make up for lost time by accelerating them in one or two performing arts areas. *Again, every transfer student is unique, and placement in the program is on a case-by-case basis.* Always confirm with an institution regarding this placement before placing your deposit!

A Few Notes on Financial Aid

First, a disclaimer: I am not a college financial aid professional. I do, however, field a lot of questions and scenarios regarding financial aid in my position, and there are a number of areas I can address.

- First, it's important for parents and students to understand the types of aid that make up the official financial aid package from a college or university. For US citizens or residents—those with a social security number—there are two avenues of aid: need-based aid and merit aid. Need-based aid can only be allocated to a student by filing the Free Application for Federal Student Aid (FAFSA). This aid consists of loans and grants and is based on a family's financial profile and ability to pay the college's total cost of attendance. Some institutions use additional applications, like the College Scholarship Service (CSS) profile, but most use only the FAFSA.

- Filing the FAFSA is not required, but I highly recommend it. Some families claim they "won't get anything" by filing the FAFSA, and I always counter that everyone should file, regardless of what outcome they expect. Each college uses the FAFSA's Estimated Family Contribution (EFC) slightly differently, based on their own fees. In the end a family is never forced to accept any form of aid—they are simply offerings. Details regarding types of loans and grants offered should always be discussed with a financial aid professional.

- The other form of aid comes in the way of merit or talent or, in other words, your scholarship. At many colleges like Pace, these awards are given based on your academic application and in the case of the talent award, your audition, and don't require a separate application. These awards can be one-year grants or one-time awards or, most often, renewable for four years provided you maintain the minimum GPA requirement. International students may or may not qualify for these awards; at Pace, an international student must have submitted the SAT or ACT scores to be eligible for the merit award but not to be awarded for talent. Again, not all institutions award the same way so it's wise to ask your admission or financial aid counselor.

The In-Person, On-Campus Experience

On its own, applying to college is a costly process. Applying to schools with a required audition adds even more expenses with travel. And then there is visiting a potential school you never knew existed until a friend at your summer intensive mentioned it. How do you fit all that into your limited schedule and/or budget? Like this whole process, there is no one right way to approach campus visits and auditions. But there are a few helpful scheduling tips I can offer you and your team to use while deciding how you tackle this giant part of the puzzle.

Visiting Schools

Most students will visit their top schools before the application and audition process. This visit can help determine whether the school will be a good fit *for you*, both academically and socially. No matter how "great" or prestigious the program, if it's not a good fit for you, then don't waste your time and money applying. However, every audition season I learn of many instances where a student has applied to more than fifteen schools. While it is certainly not a bad idea, given the selectivity of Musical Theater programs around the country, it's rarely possible to be able to visit all of them. Thus, I'll give suggestions based on what parents and students typically do in this scenario.

First, map out a plan for visiting as many as fiscally and reasonably possible. If scheduling the trips during the fall of your senior year, try to avoid using too many of your allotted high school absences because you'll need them in the winter/spring for auditions! *The summer before your senior year* can be a great time to visit—no school to miss, the weather is better for travel, and so on—but you won't see the school "in action" like you will in the fall term. Also, some schools will let you observe both academic and performing arts classes if your visit coincides with the semester. As you plan, be sure to ask their policy on this!

Alternatively, there are those schools that you've never visited—and maybe never even applied to!—but you discover them at, say, Unifieds in Chicago or Los Angeles and they admit you. In the end, you need to at least try to visit any serious contender in your college search that has admitted you. Having numerous college choices in March and April is a great thing but choosing a college that you've never even seen is a pretty risky venture.

> **Tip 1**: Don't forget the other schools that might be in the area or convenient to your "tour." If you are close, stop by, especially if you know very little about the school. You might find a gem along the way!

Scheduling the Audition

Since every school has a different way of scheduling the audition, I won't try to summarize in any one way—except to say: SCHEDULE EARLY. Most college auditions take place December through February, so prospective teams should be putting together their own audition schedules by November. For colleges that prescreen their applicants, like Pace, the scheduling happens rather automatically.

One great advantage to the prescreen platform that we use at Pace—Acceptd—is that a student who passes the prescreen can be automatically scheduled. Basically, the Acceptd application that each student submits acts as not only an audition file for the college, but also the scheduling assistant to communicate and confirm the student's preselected audition date.

For some teams, managing the audition schedule can be the most frustrating. While both the auditioning teams and the individual programs strive to maintain an uninterrupted audition calendar, forces of nature can cause chaos—especially in the winter months when most auditions are held. Cancelled flights, poor travel conditions, family emergencies, and a busy senior year are common occurrences. Pace, like most colleges, offers a certain degree of flexibility with advance notice—and sometimes even without it. The earlier that you know of a conflict, the easier it is to reschedule the audition. For conflicts that arise only days before, however, this can be tricky, especially if you are scheduled for one of the last auditions. I always tell students to select early audition dates so that in the instance of a conflict or inclement weather, there are still later options to attend. Some colleges will accept video auditions in lieu of the in-person audition and others will not.

Some families will need to book multiple auditions in a single weekend in order to maximize on time and money spent in one location. In these cases, always check with each college to know the duration of each audition. Some colleges will give you a block of time and others will have specific time slots. Knowing your exact time will allow you the ability to plan travel from college to college. At large audition events such as the National Unified Theater Auditions, this becomes even more crucial. At Pace, there is always a bit of down time as we see monologues and songs individually, while the dance call requires all to be present. This can affect the timing of your full audition, depending on where you fall in the rotation. Again, check with each college to see if there will be time for you to complete another, shorter audition the same day. Colleges tend to be flexible with this, and you should never hesitate to ask the person or persons running the audition. One note, though: be mindful that each college takes great care in designing its audition—so be respectful of all aspects of the audition and be sure to complete all components!

Chapter Takeaway

Those Devilish Details

The application process is extensive and sometimes complicated, but as with everything else so far, it is manageable in smaller units. The best advice I can offer you and your team is to read everything very carefully and keep a detailed checklist of what is required at each school, as well as your progress toward fulfilling those requirements. Checklists and charts will keep you organized and informed, as all the information will be in one place. Stay ahead of the deadlines and ask questions as necessary. Remember, the enrollment faculty and staff are there to help you succeed in this process, so utilize their expertise, but remember to be respectful of their time.

7 | "Look at Me Now"

PRESCREENS

We have done prescreens for around five years now; take advantage of the opportunity. I encourage students to prescreen for ten to fifteen schools. If you get invites from everyone, you are on the right track and will likely get in somewhere. If you get a lot of rejections in the prescreen phase, it gives you an opportunity to adjust your package and expand your reach by submitting to more schools.

—Matt Edwards, Associate Professor and Coordinator of Musical Theatre Voice, Shenandoah University

What Is a Prescreen?

A prescreen is a digital audition that is most frequently administered by a third-party web-based platform that helps schools manage and track all applicants who are auditioning. On the website of these platforms, you upload videos of your audition material, presenting them as you would in a live audition.

You need to think of this step as your first audition for the program. If you pass your prescreen and move on to a live audition, you should think of that as a callback. You must prepare for your prescreen the same as you would for a live audition: it is just as important. It is also our first impression of you. Make sure you follow all of the requirements, label the files correctly, and double-check that you are presenting everything the way you intend.

Something to also consider is that we go back to the prescreen submissions as we make the final decisions. We refer to them constantly to remind us of you and your skill set, another reason they need to be a true representation of who you are and what you do.

> **Tip 1:** You'd be surprised what we see in these video submissions, so I implore you to use common sense and watch and retape until you feel like you have a prescreen that truly represents you.

Why Do So Many Schools Use Prescreens?

- It helps the programs manage numbers. Some schools can get up to two thousand prescreen videos. Prescreens and the corresponding websites help to keep track of each student in a way that is accessible and manageable for recruitment personnel and the auditors.
- It saves money. Auditions are expensive, both for the universities recruiting and for the families auditioning. By using the prescreen video as a first step, families can save on travel, and on the university end, it can save on operation costs.
- As stated above, it becomes an invaluable reference when the auditors make final decisions. Once we are at the stage that we are making our final decisions, many schools will watch the prescreen of those at the top to ensure we are confident with our decision. It is a great way to get a sense of your skill, technique, look, and essence. These videos become an incredible reference for everyone too, as not all faculty attend the same auditions. Some schools even hire outside audition panels, and the videos become a lifeline to connect all the comments and notes among the many auditors.
- It helps recruitment staff. These important people manage and schedule your live auditions and communicate with you about requirements and deadlines. Through the web platforms, you can ask questions, schedule your on-campus auditions directly, and ensure that you have all of your material submitted. The instructions are easy to find and will guide you through the process seamlessly.
- It gives us more time in the room with the candidate. The math is simple: the fewer people we see, the more time we have in the room to get to know you as a person and performer.
- It gives you the opportunity to record and re-record until you have gotten it right. During live auditions, you only have one shot, but with video you have unlimited do-overs!

Reasons Some Schools Do Not Use Prescreens

- Poor video quality can affect our ability to assess talent. If there are obstructions in your video—such as poor picture or sound quality, a bad camera angle, or bad lighting—it can really affect how some auditors see and assess you. This is an important reason to make sure that your video is a clear representation of you so your skill, talent, and personality can shine through.
- Some colleges prefer to be in the same space as each candidate to get a sense of their personality rather than assessing it through a screen. We can't deny this is true, but often times it is a matter of resources on the university's end, not a personal preference of the auditors.
- Recordings can feel more mechanical and remote, with no opportunity to make or give adjustments. Many times during the live audition, we will ask for additional material or for you to make an adjustment to your acting or vocal technique in one of your presented songs or monologues. How an actor takes adjustments can be very important to how we assess skill and talent. Obviously, you can't do that in a video format.
- With no limit to the number of video submissions, prescreens feel like double the amount of work for the auditors. We can often see up to one hundred hours' worth of prescreens, and to do that as well as live auditions can take a great deal of the faculty's time. Each school that uses prescreens has their way of identifying who watches the video submissions. For Pace, only one faculty member is assigned to this task, ensuring the assessment is consistent. Furthermore, in addition to the added time for those who watch the videos, it potentially costs the university more money to have faculty prescreen.

Creating the Prescreen

If the program you apply to requires a prescreen video, here is what you will need:

- A good camera. At this point, cell phones have quality cameras and creating your video on your phone is a great option.
- A stand to hold your camera. Ideally, the camera should be stationary so the picture is as still as possible.

- Someone to operate the camera. It is helpful to have someone start and stop the recording so you are in place and ready to sing from the beginning of the video. Also, if you plan to move a lot, it can help to have someone operate the camera so they can move with you.
- Someone to play the piano or start the recording of your track. It can be awkward to start your own music as it may take you out of the frame of the camera. If you can, find someone to play the piano or press play on the recording. The filming will look much smoother and you will present the most confident and relaxed you.

Applicants submit their first audition for our program via video recording. You do not need to hire a professional videographer, but do be aware of your surroundings. You don't want your pets walking through the shot, or someone preparing dinner in the background. Also, minimize background noise as much as you are able and make sure you are well lit. A small but worthwhile investment is an external microphone for your video recording device. Having a microphone closer to you, that is of higher quality than most built-in microphones on phones/cameras/tablets can make a big difference in the quality of your recording.

—Jason Debord, Assistant Professor of Music,
Department of Musical Theatre, University of Michigan

What about Cost and Equipment?

There is no need to spend a lot of money to film your prescreen (or any money for that matter, if you don't want to). A cell phone with a decent camera should be enough to get a good quality video. Sure, you could get a professional videographer in a studio with expensive microphones and a grand piano, but I can promise you that will not give you an edge up. A clean video that sounds clear and follows the advice below should be all that you need to make the right kind of first impression.

The two most popular web-based platforms that schools use for prescreen auditions are Acceptd and SlideRoom. They are very user-friendly and guide you step-by-step through the process of uploading your videos. They also include helpful tutorials on what to do and, sometimes more importantly, what not to do. Before you are ready to upload, spend time on their websites so that you can get a sense of how they work and what they can do.

Most of the third-party websites will have a fee, which is often included in the application/audition fee for the university program. You can typically pay these fees all at once on the site.

> **Tip 2:** Each program you audition for will have an application fee. Be aware that costs can rack up very quickly as you apply.

If you are worried about the fees for prescreen auditions, you can contact the university and see if they have any need-based fee waivers. If not, think of it this way: it is considerably less expensive to make a good video than it is to fly across the country, rent a car, and stay in a hotel to audition live. You will know soon after you submit the video if you will have an in-person audition, and you can then start managing travel costs. I believe it is much more respectful to go through this first step before asking your family to spend a considerable amount of money on a live audition trip. Especially when the program may not even be interested in you in the first place. This may sound harsh but it's true.

More Tips for Prescreens

- Dress like you are auditioning live. Just because this is a prescreen audition, it doesn't mean you should wear your high school uniform or sweats. This is our very first impression of you, so make it a good one. You may wear the same thing for your prescreen as you do in your live audition if you want, but it is not at all required or necessary.
- Find a natural space in which to record with good acoustics and check the balance. Your bathroom, a stairwell, or the school gym—these are terrible places to film because they tend to be too "live" or too resonant. Your choir room or your voice teacher's studio work well.
- Be in the frame of the camera and keep it steady. This means that your camera should be on a stationary stand or platform aimed at the proper height. Have someone help you film your audition if you can, and make sure your head is not cut off, you are in focus, and so forth.
- Find a space to record that has complimentary lighting. Natural light is great if possible. If the room is too dark (or too bright), you may look distorted or we won't be able to see your acting. You want to put your best self forward.
- Find a space that does not have too much clutter. If you have no other space and need to use your bedroom or another room in your house, make sure it is neat. Make your bed and pick your clothes up off the floor. A messy room will distract us from watching you. Remember, you are inviting us into your home.
- Make sure that each video is properly labeled and marked. You would be surprised how many clips are labeled incorrectly or not

labeled at all. I expect the name of the video to correspond with the song or monologue that is being performed. It tells me about the kind of student you are, or might be, if this step is not done correctly. It only takes seconds to make sure they match, and it can help us tremendously.

- Humanize your slate. You are welcome to "slate" or introduce each piece with a statement like "Hi, everyone, thanks for watching. My first piece is 'I Wish I Were in Love Again' from *Babes in Arms*." You can give us your name in each slate, but we really don't need it. And because the slate can help us learn about you as well, feel free to share some of your personality and humanity with us. By humanity I mean simply let us see you, who you really are. You are not a robot, but some slates come off that way. Bring in your joy and light and a sense of openness. After you slate, please take a brief second to breathe before you start your song or monologue.

- Your audition selections should NOT all be in one clip unless that format is specifically requested. You will be prompted to upload your videos in separate windows. Please follow the instructions and do not upload your songs and monologue in one long clip. They should be broken down and labeled. It is more difficult for us to search through your material if it is all in one long clip.

- Where do I look? I prefer for you to not look directly into the camera. Slate to the camera, but put your "scene partner," the person you are talking/singing to, just to the right or left of the camera. If you are auditioning for an acting on film/TV program, they may prefer that you directly address the camera, but because most of the programs you will be auditioning for will be theater-based, it is often more effective if you don't talk to the camera.

- File format: Check the website for its preferred file format. Most will require an MP4, the most common video format, but the platform you use will tell you if it requires something different. This will happen rarely as MP4 is the most common and easy to create.

- Aspect ratio: Make sure the aspect ratio is set to standard, not wide screen. This is a function of your camera and can be easily adjusted. A computer screen is not set up to easily accommodate different viewing formats and your video could become distorted if filmed in the wide-screen mode. Like I said above, we want to see you at your best.

What about a Dance Video?

Some schools will require a dance component in the prescreen requirements and others will not. Some will even give you specific choreography to learn and perform as the dance submission. Those that do will be very specific with what they want you to film, so make sure that you read (and re-read) the instructions carefully. Schools that require a dance prescreen are looking to assess your dance skill equally with your singing and acting skill. Some may want to see how comfortable you are in your body and others want to see how you handle style. If the dance video is optional and you are not a confident dancer, don't film a dance video. It is optional for a reason, so why post something that you are not spectacular at if you don't have to? Like I've said before, you always want to present your best self in this initial audition.

Filming Tips for Dance

Dance videos can be awkward to film because of how much you move and the fact that there are typically mirrors in your dance space, but hopefully these tips will help:

- Perform *TO* the camera (not the mirrors) if possible. Make the camera your audience. It can be distracting to watch the back of you and the front of you in a mirror. It also can be hard to capture all of you in the shot with the angle required to film into the mirror. Ask a friend or parent to help you with this video so they can help angle the camera toward you as you move through the space.
- Find a space that allows you to have a full body shot. Record your dance video in a studio, a large rehearsal room, or even on a stage if possible. Filming dance requires depth between the camera and performer to ensure that your whole body will be in the shot. We want to see your technique *and* your emotion.
- Dance in a style that suits you best. Are you a fierce tap dancer but struggle with ballet? Can you completely embody a character with your movement but fall out of double pirouettes? Have you been dancing since you were three and can kick your face, as they say? Show us what you can do, not what you can't. Musical Theater uses a range of dance techniques, and we are always looking for individuals with a variety of dance skills.

- Don't include others. We are looking for a solo clip. Sometimes we will get group videos from a recital or competition with a comment that says, "I'm third from the right in pigtails." Don't make the faculty work to follow you in a crowd or allow them to compare you to the others in the video. The comparison may not come out in your favor.
- If you are asked for specific requirements, make sure you follow the instructions. If the program requests to see a battement, a double pirouette, and a grand jeté, include them in your video. You can still incorporate your own style, but if you don't show them what they want to see, it won't matter how good you are at everything else.

Tip 3: Remember that if you have the option to not submit a dance video and you don't dance . . . *don't dance.*

Supplementary Material/Wild Card

Some schools will give you the option of uploading a wild card or other supplementary material. I really encourage you to add this submission if you have the choice, as it is a great chance for us to meet you in a different way. The wild card can be anything, such as telling us a story, singing in a different style, explaining why we are the right school for you, showing a special skill, or even baking a cake with time laps. Be creative and look at this as a chance for us to get to know you better. I find these wild card videos extremely beneficial because it gives us another glimpse of you and your personality. We hope you will have fun with them too. Supplementary material can be letters of recommendation, essays, or some kind of portfolio that adds another dimension to your audition package as well.

Bob Cline, New York casting director and adjunct professor at Pace University, watches the thousands of prescreen videos we receive each year. After seeing so many auditions, both on screen and in person, he has a few great pieces of advice for you as you prepare and submit your videos:

- *It is often easier to pass through a program's prescreen audition before they have their first in-person audition days. I don't want to rush you, and by all means, if you are not ready, wait and submit your best video when it is ready. But know that once we begin to see people in the room, there is a good chance we will fall in love with a few, and they will set the bar for both prescreen and in-person auditions for the rest of the season.*

- *Contrasting Songs can mean many things. Some people, women especially, think this means they should belt one song, and then sing one legit - or in their soprano - when maybe one of those isn't necessarily their strongest option. Instead, maybe belt or mix both an up-tempo and a ballad. That is still considered a contrasting audition package. Or perhaps do a comedy song and a more dramatic piece, in whatever voice placement works best for you. The point is, there are many ways to be contrasting, so find the way that suits you and your voice best. It makes me sad when I adore the first audition clip, and then I'm crushed by the second song because it's not something they do well, rather, it's what they thought we wanted to see. Sing what you love, don't try to guess what we might want to see. What we want to see is you at your best, doing what you love to do.*

- *Last thing. Besides the monologue and song selections, some programs allow you to submit optional dance clips or wildcard videos. I have to recommend that you attempt at least one of them, if not both. Why not make me laugh? Show me you have good ideas and instincts, or that you would be great or even fun to work with. Let me know that you are the type of person I'd want to add into the mix of current students I'm already enamored with. Or even take a risk and laugh at yourself and this odd way you have to get into college.*

Chapter Takeaway

Do's and Don'ts for a Better Prescreen

Do: Upload each individual clip separately and label them properly.

Don't: Put all the requirements in one long clip.

Do: Make sure you look like you are auditioning. Brush your hair and put on an outfit that makes you look like you care . . . a lot. This is our first impression of you. Make it a good one.

Don't: Wear sweatpants, your high school sweatshirt, your uniform, pajamas, or a costume.

Do: Make sure you follow the audition requirements. Each school will most likely ask for something just slightly different (which we know is annoying and stressful for you), so pay attention to the specifics for each program.

Don't: Upload your mom's video footage of you in your production of *Cabaret*. We need to see how you audition, not how you play a role. Often there is a section where you can upload additional material, and you are welcome to upload that footage there.

Do: Make sure you are centered in the middle of the shot and that we can see at least three-quarters of your body.

Don't: Film your prescreen outside . . . or in the bathroom . . . or in the hallway . . . or in your messy room. I promise you that the acoustics in the bathroom are not right for an audition video. If you do need to tape in your bedroom, then make your bed.

Do: Act the songs as if you were auditioning live.

Don't: Use props, your home furniture as set pieces, or your friends as scene partners.

Remember: You may feel that the prescreen is cold and informal, but at the end of the day it can save you time, money, and energy. Take pride in your prescreen. Be thoughtful and creative, and realize that it is the very first impression we have of you. It is easy to make it a good one!

8 | "Another Hundred People"
NATIONAL UNIFIED AUDITIONS

Try and stay as open and relaxed as possible. We are here to get to know you and to support you. Try and make this a fun experience. We want you to succeed!
—Barbara MacKenzie-Wood, Raymond W. Smith Professor of Acting,
Carnegie Mellon University, School of Drama

Tip 1: It is important to start by saying that Unifieds don't have a centralized source. You can't go to one site, or call one person, to register or get questions answered. Each school and program is in charge of its own audition at Unifieds. Therefore, you will need to contact each program directly and individually to schedule your audition time and ask any questions. This can be extremely frustrating, but knowing this upfront will help.

What Are They?

The Unified auditions are a collection of university theater programs from around the country that gather in the same location over a weekend to audition and interview perspective theater majors. Unifieds are held in New York, Los Angeles, and Chicago. These auditions are usually held in a hotel, and each school uses a large conference room specifically dedicated to their individual auditions—there are no multischool audition calls, thought I have heard of a few schools who share a dance call. Some schools may attend the Unified weekend but not use the Unified audition site. Instead they will rent a separate space, such as a local dance studio or a small theater. Each program wants you to access their audition without difficulty, so it is likely that the secondary location will be close to the hotel so you can get to and from each audition with ease.

> **Tip 2:** It is not only Musical Theater programs that audition at Unifieds. BFA acting, design, and film programs, as well as BA programs, are all included.

Approximately twenty-five theater programs audition at Unifieds. Some schools may not be at every Unified city and there are many programs that do not use the Unified auditions at all. If you choose to audition this way, do your best to pick a location that has all the schools you are interested in. What can also complicate things is that still other programs that are not a part of the Unified auditions will hold their own separate auditions in the same city on the same weekend. For example, it would not make sense for New York City schools to hold auditions at the New York Unifieds when their campuses are so near. They will, however, hold their own on-campus auditions the same weekend as the Unifieds, so you can still make a single trip to New York City for all your different program auditions.

The big draw of the Unified auditions is that all the schools on your college list might be at the Chicago location, and you could potentially audition for every program at once if you wanted. Auditioning for eight to ten programs individually is very expensive, and going to one location can be an economical way to go about it. As stated above, one of the drawbacks to the Unified format is that there is no central way to sign up to audition for every program attending any given Unified audition; you will still need to speak with the individual admission offices for each school to schedule an audition time. And, though that longer process might feel overwhelming, there are definite plusses and minuses to auditioning through Unifieds.

But Is It Right for Me?

Pros

- Cost Savings

There is no question that auditioning at Unifieds can be the most economical way to go about the audition process. One airplane ticket, one hotel room, and you often don't even need to rent a car. You will still need to pay all of the application fees required by the individual schools, but this way can really consolidate travel costs. Once you are accepted, you can always visit the campus and pay for a separate flight then.

- Efficiency

I recommend that you have eight to twelve schools on your list. If planned right, you can audition for all of them in one weekend. You may be tired, but being able to enjoy the fact that you have done what you needed to do in just a few days, rather than spread it out over a number of weeks can be worth it.

- Senior Year

Your senior year of high school is an intense time, and a lot is asked and required of you. Unlike the first three years of high school, you suddenly have endless obligations outside of your course load. Shows, competitions, exams, recitals, concerts, games—those are not on the "audition schedule" and it is important to realize that you may miss some of these commitments for your college auditions. Especially if you go to a school where the counselors and teachers are unfamiliar with the college theater audition process, they may not understand why you need to miss so much school to fly halfway across the country to attend auditions. It is up to you to educate your school about what's involved in your process. At least with Unifieds, you can consolidate the process into one trip.

- Community

You have the opportunity to make a lot of new friends during Unifieds; it is a great way to develop community. Navigating this process with people who truly understand what you are going through is priceless. You all are in the same place, with the same dream, the same stress, and the same shared passion: you already have so much in common. The same is true of whoever goes along with you. Parents, mentors, teachers, and friends often find this is a great way to meet people with similar experiences. If you are coming with a parent, I find that it is very helpful for parents to talk to other parents. Believe it or not, this is a stressful time for them too, and having other people to talk to is very helpful for them.

- School Comparisons

Having the auditions so close together (typically, you will leave one audition and walk right into another in the next room down the hall) can really help you assess not only the work you did, but also the vibe and energy of each school. This can prove very helpful in seeking out programs that are the "right fit" for you.

- Dance Call

Not every school will hold a dance call at Unifieds. Some schools don't bring their dance faculty, don't have the space in the hotel to hold the call, or, frankly, don't prioritize a dance call in the selection of their class. If a dance call is not offered at Unifieds, but dance is really your thing, then you may want to do that specific audition on campus. Be aware that by necessity a dance call at Unifieds may be on carpet in a hotel ballroom. Again, some programs will rent additional space outside the designated hotel so that they can utilize a more traditional dance/audition space, but that isn't always an option for the school. It's best to always confirm the details with each school.

- Walk-ins

Some schools at Unifieds offer walk-in auditions. The procedures for these vary by school, and the programs that offer walk-ins will vary from site to site, and year to year. If you have spare time between auditions, you may wish to try your hand at a walk-in if a program intrigues you. Some schools will allow you to walk in without applying or paying for an audition and then let you know if you should proceed with your application afterward. However, you should never count on walk-ins being available for a particular school, especially if that school is one of your top-tier choices. And if a program is very popular, it may not have time to see any walk-ins. Remember: it is always better to have a scheduled audition on the books than to risk not getting one at all.

- Students, Parents, and Alumni

Many schools will invite local parents, students, or alumni to help at Unifieds. You might see a parent of a current student checking you in. You might see an alumnus sitting at the table with the auditor. You might see a successful alum teaching the dance call. While you're waiting for your turn, use the time to ask them about their experiences with the program. You will not find a better or more truthful resource. You won't get parents or alumni at the on-campus events. I view this as a major plus!

Cons

We don't audition at Unifieds. Students can be so overwhelmed by the many schools there that it's hard to get their attention. There's only so much "bandwidth" to go around. Students can get their hearts set on a dream school, or a school they've heard or read is good, and they'll skip appointments with other schools, or be distracted. I prefer to meet students at auditions where they're really focused on the experience of meeting me, getting to know my school, and finding out if it's a good fit. I do some private group auditions and some auditions at performing arts schools we have established relationships with. Always a better experience.

—Joe Deer, Chair, Department of Theatre, Dance, and Motion Pictures, and Director of the Musical Theatre Initiative, Wright State University

- What If?

You plan to do all of your auditions at once, at a single Unifieds, and you get sick. Things just became quite problematic for you. The same is true if the weather is bad and your flight is canceled (why Unifieds are in Chicago in February, nobody knows). Most schools will accommodate you if something like this comes up, but there is no guarantee. This is a small risk you take when auditioning in this all-or-nothing way.

- Tracks

Most of the time at Unifieds you will audition with recorded tracks and not live piano accompaniment. As a reminder, a "track" *is the recorded accompaniment that you use to sing your audition songs.* You will also have to bring something to play your track, and sometimes walking in with your speakers, iPad, CD (or whatever you are using), can feel clunky and a bit awkward. My advice is to bring small Bluetooth speakers (if you are able) that can connect to your phone, iPad, or computer so you eliminate any tangled chordography in the room. You want to make sure that you have your tracks hyperorganized so you can easily get to what you need. Often times you will also need to press play for yourself. As long as you are aware of all of this and make your time in the room easy, fun, and light, you should be fine. We understand: we would all prefer live accompaniment, but sometimes it is just not an option.

- Not on Campus

Because the auditions take place in a hotel, you are not able to meet students, see the campus, or sit in on classes. Being on campus, meeting the students and faculty, and seeing the faculty teach are all invaluable, especially when making your final decisions on where to attend. You don't get that chance at Unifieds. This also means that you are not auditioning in traditional audition spaces. You could be dancing in a hotel ballroom on carpet or singing in a conference room with no soundproofing. We just don't have the kind of control that we would have on campus. Not that this is bad, but it is just a factor to consider.

> **Tip 3:** You truly should not attend a school that you have never seen. On-campus auditions are usually run at least partially by the students of the program. Talking with them and listening to their experiences is a great way to get a feeling of the place and the community.

- Who You Are Auditioning For

Many times, the full faculty that does the on-campus auditions will not be at Unifieds. Cost to the university, teaching schedules, rehearsal schedules, and other factors can prevent them from attending. Sometimes the programs will even hire outside professionals to attend these auditions in lieu of sending the faculty. This really should not matter, but it is something you may want to consider. Trust that each school has a very clear and transparent policy for how they assess each person, and whoever is behind the table should share that exact policy.

- Soooooo Many Musical Theater People

You will be staying in a hotel with (often) lots of *very* high energy, *very* loud, *very* passionate college hopefuls. Most Musical Theater kids LOVE this, but the experience can sometimes be overwhelming because there are so many of you doing the same thing at the same time. It is easy to get distracted, so it is your job to find a way to stay fully focused. If you know what it's like to be in a show or summer camp, where you are only surrounded by Musical Theater types . . . just magnify that by one hundred.

- Hyperorganization

Every program will ask for something slightly different. Add to that the possibility that you may be auditioning for different types of programs (BFA, BA, BFA acting, BMus) in a single day. You need a very clear system to ensure you are presenting the correct material to the correct program at each school's audition within the larger Unifieds, as well as the material needed for the programs auditioning over the weekend outside of the official Unifieds. Also, don't forget proper dancewear and shoes if any of your auditions include a dance call.

- Speed

At Pace, we have eight different on-campus audition days, Michigan has six, and Boston Conservatory has nine. Compare that to the two or three total audition days at Unifieds, often with a program seeing a similar number of students in those fewer days. This can mean that the auditions might move faster, or your allotted time might be shorter, than if you were on campus. This does not make a difference to us on the program end, but it may make a difference in how you feel about your audition.

- Not as Independent

When you audition on campus, you leave whoever brought you (parent, friend, mentor, etc.) at some point during the process. Typically, this happens soon after you are checked in. They are asked to stay in a waiting room, they may get their own campus tour, or they are asked to leave and not come back until a certain time. At Unifieds, there isn't anyone telling your parents where to go and what to do, and this can mean that they are quite literally in your space the whole time. This can be even more nerve-wracking than the auditions themselves. If you are accompanying your student to Unifieds, please heed this advice: *Let your kid be.* Give them room. Find other parents and go somewhere together—the hotel bar or a restaurant—and learn from each other. It's possible that you could make friends out of this experience too. If you are hovering, it has the potential to make your child more anxious and possibly even stress them out more than they already are. No matter how close you are, they really need space at these auditions. This is the time for them to test out their independence and take ownership of this process. I heard a story of a parent (let's call him Mr. Parent) listening with his ear to the door of his child's (let's call him Kyle) audition. Kyle specifically said to Mr. Parent that he wanted to do this on his own and would come find him in their room when the audition was over. Mr. Parent gave Kyle a hug and went around the corner. Kyle went into the audition room and then Mr. Parent came out from behind the corner and put his ear to the door to listen. After the first song, Kyle realized that he forgot something he needed out in the hallway and opened the door to find Mr. Parent standing right in front of him. It threw Kyle off that Mr. Parent didn't honor his wish for Mr. Parent to go back to the room, and when Kyle went back in to the audition room, he couldn't shake it, and he tanked. Let your child take the lead and follow that with respect.

There is no evidence to suggest that there is an acceptance difference auditioning on campus or at Unifieds. What is great about the Unified auditions is that they give you convenient options during this hectic and expensive process. You will decide what is best for you and your family, but just remember that they exist and can be very helpful.

The Attendee Perspective

Attending Unifieds can be overwhelming, even for the most prepared student. There are hundreds of teenagers and parents all gathered in a single hotel vying for a chance to "get in" to as many schools as possible. This could be a nightmare for some, but it can also be exciting and fun too; there are as many Unified experiences as there are people who attend them. But I wanted to give you an idea of how the weekend can go, from a student and a parent perspective, to help demystify the weekend.

The Student Experience: Leana

While everyone has their own opinion of the Unified auditions, I thoroughly enjoyed my experience at the Chicago Unifieds; it was my first taste of independence in the theater world. I was lucky enough to have my mother traveling with me to each audition city throughout the process, but when we arrived in Chicago, something inside said, "I got this!" and I let my mom relax as I went from audition to audition.

Not only did Unifieds give me a sense of independence and responsibility, but also it gave me five days of feeling so incredibly inspired. I was surrounded by so many talented and kind artists, and I even met one of my now best friends at our Pace dance call. It's easy to think that everyone will be mean and competitive, but I actually found that the people I interacted with were just as excited as I was. We were all going through the same process, so why not make some friends along the way? Besides, no matter where we all eventually wound up, these people would someday be my colleagues in the professional world.

If there are two things I wish I knew going into this process they would be, one, audition fatigue is a real thing. By day five of Unifieds, I was sick as a dog and quite literally couldn't sing above an A. I'm not sure if there is any way to ensure that this doesn't happen, but I wish I had put all of my "priority" schools at the beginning of the week instead of at the end. And, two, I wish there had been someone to reassure me that I do have a place in this world of Musical Theater, and most likely, I would end up exactly where I was meant to be. Even if that place was the exact opposite of what I thought I wanted, it is what I needed.

The Parent Experience: Danielle

> **Tip 4:** Students, your parents/team aren't going to know what to do for this long weekend, and they are going to want to help you as much as possible; it's what they do. But it's okay to set expectations of how much help you think you'll want while auditioning, and how much space you'll need.

One of the unique experiences of the college audition year is attending "Unifieds" at one of the National Unified audition sites. I always tell people it's sort of like landing on "Planet Glee," with hundreds of kids just like yours, and a lot of stressed-out parents, just like you. Colleges from all over the country set up shop in various hotel ballrooms and meeting rooms to hold in-person auditions while the moms and dads sweat it out nervously in the lobbies. Most of the auditions require your kid to set up appointments in advance, but some allow walk-ins.

> *Field note #1: Parents, take a stroll around the hotel and make notes of which schools are taking walk-ins in case your kid wants to give one or two a shot. This is a great use of your nervous energy!*

At Unifieds, the air is electric with nervous energy and teenage enthusiasm. It's truly a one-of-a-kind event, especially for a parent who has no background in performing. The trick is figuring out what to do while your kid is racing from audition to audition.

> *Field note #2: Find the bar (they serve coffee and tea at the bar too). The other parents will be in the bar.*

Every kid is different, but I kind of served as a combination home base and Sherpa during Unifieds. I didn't accompany them from audition to audition; rather I stayed in the lobby of the hotel in our hometown of Los Angeles, or in my hotel room when we flew to Chicago Unifieds. That way,

I was a text message away if an extra headshot or different dance shoes were needed, but I wasn't hovering over them the whole day. However, there were parents who stayed with their kids throughout the day, hopefully because their kids wanted it that way.

Field note #3: Don't be the parent with their ear pressed up against the audition room door while your kid is in the room. It makes it awkward for everyone.

While at Unifieds, it was so nice to connect with other parents who were there with their kids. I can honestly say I still stay in touch with many of the people I met at Unifieds now that our kids are working actors. We support each other's children as they come through our towns for various performances, and we are there for each other as our kids navigate their lives as actors. And it really all started in the hotel lobby and, yes, in the hotel bar at Unifieds.

Chapter Takeaway

A Unified Checklist

There is so much to remember when applying to the Unified auditions, especially knowing that you must apply to each school separately. Follow the list below to ensure that you meet all your deadlines and create a wonderful weekend.

- First, determine that your schools are participating in the Unified weekend you are attending. Every Unified city is different, and not all schools attend all cities.
- List each school in a separate column and write down the following:
  - Their audition times throughout the weekend
  - The length of the actual audition
  - The requirements of the audition—is there a dance call? An interview?
  - Are you expected to stay for the entire duration, or can you leave when finished? (this will help with timing)
  - The location of the audition—some schools will have on-campus auditions the same weekend or be in a space close to the main hotel (another timing factor)
- Once you've made this list, you can cross-reference all your prospective audition start times and durations to create a full weekend timeline, hopefully with very few overlapping or problematic times
- Using this timeline, you can confidently apply for each school's audition and ask about any possible conflicts of time you have found.
  - Remember that everyone knows how time-sensitive Unifieds are, and they will work to help make it an easy experience if you are prepared and know ahead of time how your schedule needs to work
- Once you have a confirmation, enter that into your time chart to ensure that you have applied and heard from all of your schools.
- If possible, leave an open time slot for a wildcard school that you see or hear about when you are there. You never know . . .

- Once you are at the Unified weekend, remember to treat it like you would any other in-person audition day (see chapter 11 for more information). But a few specific things to help you through the day:
  - Get enough sleep—it's going to be a long day
  - Eat a good breakfast
  - Bring snacks that are easy to eat and won't affect your voice
  - Drink water
  - Bring your timeline so you know where you need to be and when
  - Take a break from the ballroom area when needed (even if it's just to run to your room for five minutes, a small regroup can work wonders)
  - Harness the energy around you and use it to fuel your day
  - Treat each audition as a separate experience
  - Take deep breaths and ground yourself before you begin
  - Have fun!

9 | "Handful of Keys"
ASK AN ACCOMPANIST

WITH STEPHANIE LAYTON

One of the most frustrating things to watch in an audition is a student who comes in with unprepared music. This includes loose-leaf sheets of music that fall, copied music that the pianist cannot read, cuts that are not marked, the singer cannot find their second song as it's buried in their book or even in another book, etc.

—Gary Kline, Assistant Option Coordinator of Acting/Musical Theater,
Teaching Professor, Carnegie Mellon University

HELLO, DEAR READER, IT'S ME, that stranger who's sitting at the piano when you walk into an audition room. Otherwise known as (cue dramatic music) *the Accompanist*. In this chapter, I'm going to attempt to dissect the audition process from an accompanist's point of view. I hope you'll find it enlightening. As you read what follows, please keep in mind that I am just one person with an opinion, and I certainly can't claim to speak on the behalf of all accompanists. We are an opinionated bunch, so the best I can do is to try to be as diplomatic as possible.

Choosing What to Sing

(From an Accompanist's Standpoint)

If you are reading this book, you are probably preparing to audition for a college program—and, more often than not, your accompanist will be a skilled pianist from the faculty. But what if they aren't? What if the team had its top accompanist lined up but she got into a car accident en route to the studio so they had to scramble to find anyone who could play at the last minute? If you're set on singing a tricky piece, go for it—but keep in mind that you're taking a bigger risk.

Back up a second, Steph, what do you mean when you say "a tricky piece"? I mean a song that is *difficult to sight-read*. Keep in mind that I, your accompanist, might be looking at your piece for the first time, particularly when it comes to newer material. Never assume that I am familiar with all of the latest shows coming to Broadway or that I am spending my Saturday nights binge-watching YouTube videos of Andrew Lippa concerts. I'm absolutely not talking about "can" and "can't" song lists (I hate those); I'm talking about *added risk*. Below I've listed some songs in this category. Many of these examples are pieces that a seasoned player will most likely be familiar with (and may love playing!), but that doesn't mean they aren't potential nightmares for someone who has never seen them before.

- Songs with lots of time/tempo changes

  "The Light in the Piazza" (*The Light in the Piazza*)
  "Proud Lady" (*The Baker's Wife*)
  "West End Avenue" (*The Magic Show*)
  "Buddy's Blues" (*Follies*)
  "The Worst Pies in London" (*Sweeney Todd*)
  "Sunset Boulevard" (*Sunset Boulevard*)
  "Super Boy and the Invisible Girl" (*Next to Normal*)
  "The Miller's Sun" (*A Little Night Music*)

- Accompaniment that is incredibly complex or fast

  "Another Hundred People" (*Company*)
  "In These Skies" (*Ace*)
  "I Think I May Want to Remember Today" (*Starting Here, Starting Now*)
  "King of the World" (*Songs for a New World*)
  "Real Big News" (*Parade*)
  "Meadowlark" (*The Baker's Wife*)
  "The Beauty Is" (*The Light in the Piazza*)
  "Out of the Blue" (*The Wild Party*)
  "Where in the World" (*The Secret Garden*)
  "How Lucky Can You Get" (*Funny Lady*)

It also never hurts to have a "back-up piece" prepared. You'll certainly be happy you did if you start noticing that multiple actors seem upset after their auditions. Ask them what the situation was like in there, and/or listen through the door if you can. Go with your gut, and choose the song that will make you feel the most confident walking into that room.

> **Tip 1:** *"Everyone says it's bad to bring Sondheim pieces into auditions"* is something I often hear young actors say, but I find it to be an old-fashioned and uninformed generalization. Think about it: "Another Hundred People" from *Company* and "Good Thing Going" from *Merrily We Roll Along* are vastly different when it comes to accompaniment difficulty. The same goes for anything by Adam Guettel, Michael John LaChiusa, Andrew Lippa, and Jason Robert Brown. Learn to distinguish what makes a specific song easy or difficult to play, and when in doubt: ask an accompanist.

Choosing Your Cut

They want to hear a full song at your audition? Lucky you! That certainly won't always be the case, and in many situations you'll have to decide "what your cut is." Some songs are easy to shorten, and some are more challenging. Here are a few things to keep in mind when making decisions about your cut.

- Choose a Cut That Makes Sense Both Musically and Lyrically

If you are asked to do a short cut of a song, it does not mean you should try to cram in every note you can sing. *Remember: if the team needs to hear more, they will ask for it.* Creating a patchwork of your favorite measures can end up sounding disjointed, with words that don't rhyme, key changes that come out of nowhere, and sentences that don't make sense. When actors try to get too clever cutting and pasting it can seriously distract from their performance and make it more difficult for me, your accompanist, to follow.

- What Do You Want for an Introduction?

This is something a lot of actors tend to overlook, especially when dealing with short cuts. How do you want to get into your song? On a practical level, your "intro" is how you're going to find your starting pitch—so make it easy on yourself and choose something that's foolproof (especially when nerves are factored in).

On an artistic level, *your intro is your "moment before" as an actor.* What kind of musical moment will best help "launch" you into the world of your song? You've got a few options:

- A bell tone, starting pitch, or interval
- A chord or arpeggio
- A vamp
- A few measures of music—often, the two bars before you start singing work well, but not always: if you are starting on a key change, for example, the two bars leading up to your entrance might make it difficult for you to find your note (and for me to establish what key I'm playing in)

Tip 2: Keep your intros simple. I (or any accompanist) can get thrown off if the two bars you choose have an extremely complex piano riff that you need played perfectly in order to find your note. I might be able to nail the riff if it's in the middle of the song, but sometimes when I see a million notes right out the gate it is overwhelming. I might approximate it, or even botch it!

Tip 3: If you are having trouble with any of the musical terms or concepts mentioned in this chapter, see appendix A for some helpful definitions and examples.

Amy here! As I've mentioned before, each school will have its own requirements for audition song length, ranging from bars to time limits, and it can be tricky to understand what it all means. I asked a few colleagues to explain their school's guidelines to give you an idea of why it varies so much and how you can make smart choices with your audition cuts:

We ask for two 1-minute cuts (approximately) of contrasting styles/ranges for our auditions because it takes about a minute, much like with the acting monologue, to build at least a bit of a story! And I need time to see them [you, the student] and their humanity in the development of their journey through that short cut.

—Gary Kline, Assistant Option Coordinator of Acting/Musical Theater,
Teaching Professor, Carnegie Melon University

We ask for each audition selection to be a minute long, or roughly 16 bars. With standard song construction, a 16-bar cut is fairly easy to accomplish. But with some contemporary material, often times a standard 16-bar cut will not allow for the completion of the dramatic or musical idea. All phrases should be finished, rather than cobbled together in order to fulfill the requirement of a strict 16 bar.

—Hank Stratton, Assistant Professor, Acting/Musical Theater Division,
University of Arizona

I ask for a song cut based mostly on time. To ask for 16 or 32 bars of a ballad is much different than a groove-based up-tempo song. Thinking in terms of time allows the individuality of each song to be taken into consideration.

—John Simpkins, Head of Musical Theatre, Penn State University

This is one of our most misunderstood directives. We specify 32 measures (which is basically an entire traditional Gershwin-type song) but are actually interested in the intent of this rule rather than the strict adherence to it. So a false ending and coda (such as the typical ending of "Someone to Watch over Me") is fine, but auditioning students should be wary of lengthy 32-bar selections, such as some songs from Les Misérables, *in which the measures actually contain eight beats and can seem too long.*

—Roger Grodsky, Professor, Music Director, and Vocal Coach,
University of Cincinnati College-Conservatory of Music (CCM)

Finding the Right Sheet Music

Let's get one thing straight: I desperately want to play your music the way it's supposed to be played. But if you don't give me something decent to look at, I cannot do that, and we'll both end up feeling frustrated. For starters, you should **never** have to apologize for what your music looks like. That might sound like a no-brainer, but I assure you it happens all the time. Here are some common offenses.

- It's a Bad Photocopy or It's Damaged

   "I'm so sorry . . . my printer ran out of ink."

It's faded, it's blurry, parts of the music are cut off. If you have trouble reading it, so will I (especially since I may not be familiar with the piece). When people hand me sheet music like this, it comes off as disrespectful and lazy, regardless of the excuse.

- It's Handwritten

   "I'm so sorry . . . I know this is impossible to read."

If this is your situation, I suggest you look to see if you can find a printed version of the song. While some songs do only exist in handwritten form, it's very off-putting to be presented with a handwritten version of "I'll Know" from *Guys and Dolls* when I know how easy it is to find the printed version.

If, after doing your research, you're positive that there isn't a printed version out there, it might be worth paying someone to put your song into music notation software (like Finale or Sibelius), especially if you plan to use it on a regular basis. I know an actor who was always running into problems with "Grand Knowing You" from *She Loves Me* (a notoriously handwritten score) until, frustrated, he broke down and paid someone to make him a clean version and immediately noticed a huge improvement at his auditions.

- It's from a Conductor Score and Lacks a Clear Piano Reduction Part

   "I'm so sorry . . . I know there's all this extra stuff in here but you know this song, right?"

A piano conductor score is often packed with instrumental cues, vocal harmonies, and other information relevant to music directing the show. This can make it unclear what you want me to play at your audition. Another negative side effect? When each measure includes all of these extra things, it usually means less measures fit onto one page, which results in more page turns for me.

Tip 4: If you have doubts about your version of a song, or an accompanist has told you it's difficult to read, see if you can find it in a vocal selections book. Songs from these types of books are arranged specifically for piano and voice.

- You Got It Transposed

  "I'm so sorry . . . the accompanist at my last audition said some of these chords are wrong."

I'm not discouraging transposing in general. Transposition websites like Musicnotes.com can be great tools, but the results aren't always stellar. If you go this route, ask a good pianist to look at the finished product to make sure it's accurate. *Huge red flags are double sharps and double flats*—these tend to crop up when something has been transposed badly.

Be selective about the repertoire you get transposed. When it comes to songs like jazz standards and pop tunes, I'm all for it. But it really throws me off when you bring in a song I'm used to playing in a specific key because it's from a show, especially if it's somewhat difficult (for one of the reasons mentioned in the previous section). "The Old Red Hills of Home" from *Parade* is in the key of F, and men sing it in auditions on a regular basis. If you get it transposed down a couple steps and bring it in, I will give it my best shot, but there's a chance I will make some mistakes as it's not what I'm used to playing. I'll probably spend the whole time wondering why you couldn't have just picked a different song.

- It's Not the Right Version of the Song

  "But you know the Norah Jones version, right?"

Love Norah Jones doing "The Nearness of You"? The version in the Hoagie Carmichael anthology at the library probably won't be in her key or sound anything like her arrangement. The same can happen when there's been a revival of a musical on Broadway and it has been re-orchestrated. The revival score for *Kiss Me, Kate* is a lot different than the original, so if you are used to hearing the original accompaniment for "Always True to You in My Fashion," you'll want to make sure you get that version.

- It's a Rock/Pop Song That Doesn't Transfer Well to Solo Piano

  "So . . . when the last accompanist played this it sounded really lame."

If you are singing a song that's already piano-based (Lady Gaga, Elton John, Billy Joel, Randy Newman, and Carole King songs are good examples), you're probably in the clear. But if you decide you want to do something that relies heavily on other instruments, particularly drums, remember that it's never going to sound like that on the piano.

Preparing Your Music

There's nothing more baffling to me than an actor with messy sheet music falling out of a binder when they walk in. Why not take advantage of one audition component you have complete control over? Plan a trip to the office supply store, and make your music clean, specific, and easy to navigate. I promise I'm not being high maintenance; this is about you! If your sheet music is sloppy or unclear, you've upped the likelihood that I will get lost or play wrong notes and tempos.

- Put It in a Binder

It should be in good condition, with rings that fully connect. Keep ring enforcers handy (those little white donut-shaped stickers) so that all three holes in your sheet music stay intact.

Why a binder? Loose-leaf sheets can fall off of the piano or slump down, depending on the piano or keyboard music stand. Add an air-conditioner or a ceiling fan into the equation and forget about it. It is equally painful to play from a brand-new vocal selections book that won't stay open.

- Organize Your Binder

Arrange your binder (a.k.a. your "book") so that you can find songs quickly and efficiently. If someone behind the table asks "can we hear a ballad?" or "do you have 'Defying Gravity' in there by chance?," you shouldn't have to shuffle through your entire book while mumbling "I know I put it in here somewhere." You will inevitably feel awkward and might even be stopped by a creative team member saying "You know what? Never mind—we're good" if the clock ticks away for too long.

I suggest listing all of your repertoire at the front of your book—either in alphabetical order or organized by category (i.e., Golden Age, 80s Pop, Comedic, Contemporary MT). Number the songs, and then put a corresponding numbered tab on each piece of sheet music. Here's an example of how that works:

You're auditioning for Gaston in *Beauty and the Beast* so you sing "Proud Lady" from *The Baker's Wife*. The team says "Great! But now do you have anything else that's like . . . more angry?" You quickly scan your list:

"Almost Like Being in Love" (1)
"I Was Here" (2)

"Proud Lady" (3)
"Vienna" (4)
"What Is It about Her?" (5)

You then flip to tab #5 for "What Is It about Her?"

Make sure to update your table of contents as you add or remove songs.

- **Avoid Sheet Protectors**

A bold statement, I know. This tends to be a hotly debated topic in the accompanist community, but after years of hearing from both sides it seems to me that the most passionately opinionated accompanists are the ones who hate them. Reflective glare from lights is a potential problem, but even with nonglare protectors it can be a pain when the plastic pulls away from the sheet music, making it suddenly foggy to read.

I've never had a very strong opinion on the topic, but the one time a ceiling light was at just the right angle on a protector, I was definitely grateful to be playing an easy song in a low-pressure situation. I also prefer to feel paper in my hands when I have to turn pages quickly—to a nonaccompanist this might sound like a silly thing, but remember: when I'm sight-reading music and have no idea what's going to be on the next page, every little thing can make a difference.

- **Photocopy Your Music So That It Is Double-Sided**

The alternative is taping single-sided sheets back-to-back (*staples hurt!*) but I think this is another personal preference issue. The "back-to-back" version sometimes makes me paranoid that I'm grabbing two pages instead of one, because I'm so used to what a single page-turn should feel like.

- **Make Sure to Include the Basics**
  - **Tempo:** A metronome marking coupled with an adjective is my favorite thing to see at the beginning of a song. Be descriptive if you can! "Moderately" isn't nearly as helpful to me as "Heavily," "Sinister Tango," "Nervous Two," "Sweeping Waltz," or "A la *Jaws* Theme." When you convey emotions to me, it helps me to inform your performance.
  - **Your introduction:** I love it when actors write "intro" where that starts and "voice" where they plan to start singing.

- **The song title and show:** Especially when you're dealing with a cut that starts in the middle of the song. Sometimes I won't immediately recognize what song it is, even if I'm familiar with it.

- Highlight (*Yes, with an Actual Highlighter Pen!*) Important Information

You do not need to highlight every obvious key change or musical marking—I am a musician, so you can safely assume that I read music, and too much highlighter can be distracting. Here are some things I think worth highlighting (on a case-by-case basis, of course):

- **Your cut.** If you make an internal cut in your music, I like it if you highlight the end of the last measure in the first chunk and the beginning of the measure that I'm supposed to jump to.
- **Anything that happens suddenly or unexpectedly.** The big ones for me would be extreme changes in tempo/feel, key, clef, or dynamics.

- Make Sure That What I'm Looking at Is What You're Planning to Do

I don't have more than a few seconds to study your music, so you want me to be looking at *only* the information I need. If there are alternate chords written in from the cabaret you just did, I'm going to wonder if I should be playing them. If there are a lot of illegible notes from your voice teacher scribbled in, I'm going to wonder if they say something that I'm supposed to be reading.

Dumb it down, and make it impossible for me to get lost. *If you are singing alternate lyrics, write them in*—for my sake *and* yours! If I'm not looking at the words you're singing, it becomes impossible for me to help you if we get off.

- Be Thoughtful about Page-turns—Minimize Them

Your sheet music should be double-sided, unless your song is only two pages. In this case you can, and should, arrange them side-by-side in your binder. For songs that are three pages, I'm a fan of taping the third page to the side of the second one and folding it "accordion style" out of the binder. Voila! No page-turns.

If page-turns are inevitable, put thought into *where* they occur. If there's a particularly wacky key or meter change at the end of a page, DON'T make that the page turn! There is nothing more terrifying for an accompanist than flipping a page and going "Gah! Suddenly we're in B and it's cut time! What the?!" The same goes if you've made an internal cut in a song. It is much nicer for me to see what's coming, rather than frantically turning a page and being shell-shocked.

Also, I should never have to flip backward, and I should never have to turn more than one page to follow your codas and cuts. If your song or cut has repeats or codas that require me to do a lot of page-flipping gymnastics, it is *much* more likely that I will get lost or frazzled. Make my job easy by making duplicate copies of pages when necessary (and/or removing excess pages), so that I can read your music from beginning to end like a book.

Talking to Me at the Piano

When you walk through the door, I might be looking at my phone, rummaging through my bag, or drinking my coffee, but please don't take this personally. I've probably been playing auditions all day, so I might not give you a giant fanfare. No matter! Say hello (I am a human), look me in the eye, and treat me as if I am your band mate. Be friendly, but please don't touch me or try to shake hands.

Be efficient. Know where your song is in your binder (or move it to the front). Place it in front of me on the music stand, and tell me what song you're doing. If you've done your music preparation thoroughly, you shouldn't have to do much more.

• Explain Your Music to Me

A quick run-down is all you should need. Avoid trying to verbalize every little thing—that's what all of those highlights and musical notations take care of! I would always point out where you've made internal cuts, even if they are clearly marked. Personally, I appreciate the additional heads-up.

• Give Me the Tempo

If your cut starts with an ad lib verse, you shouldn't need to explain this— if I see "Colla Voce," "Ad Lib," "Rubato," or "Freely," I know to follow you. Take me to the chorus or a part of the song that is in tempo, and im- agine yourself singing it. Do something physical like tapping on your leg, your shoulder, or your hand. *Don't rush or feel like you need to apologize for taking time for this.* I can tell that a lot of actors hate this part because they feel stupid, but it's important to get comfortable with it. Sing quietly (this is not your audition yet!), and stop singing as soon as I say, "Okay, got it!"

Tip 5: Think about how you're going to talk to me ahead of time, but don't be surprised if I "break from the script." If I know your song, I might immediately say *"Oh, this song! Got it,"* which means that I don't need any more information from you (unless you plan to do something out-of-the-ordinary with it). If I'm not familiar with your song or I'm confused by something, I'll ask you more questions.

Your Audition

Unless you specified something at the piano with me in advance, I will start playing your introduction when you look like you're ready. Do not assume that I am going to wait for a head nod or a breath just because that's what the accompanist in your last audition class did. *If you want me to wait for a specific cue, you need to tell me in advance.*

During your song, take the lead and don't be passive. Drive the train. If it feels too fast, slow down a bit and I will follow you. If it feels too slow, push it and hopefully I'll get the memo. You know the song and I might not, so don't expect me to read your mind.

If early on (within the first several bars) you realize that we are totally not together or something is really wrong, it is okay to stop and start again if you do it with grace. *Do not throw me under the bus*—"that sounded wrong" or "this is way too slow"—*even if you know it was my fault.* Take the blame entirely or make it a collaborative fix—"I'm sorry, I gave that tempo to you way too fast because I was excited" or "Can we try that again a little faster?" I know that seems unfair, but the way you handle the situation has the potential to either endear you to the team or turn them off completely. Keep in mind that they may not have even noticed that something was going wrong when you stopped, so acting annoyed might just make you seem difficult or high-maintenance. As a side note (and maybe I'm in the minority here in Accompanist Land), if something was my fault I always own up to it—"no, that was my bad—I totally spaced out"—and then you look like a total saint for taking the hit.

Remember, even if your sheet music is in great shape, *I might make a mistake.* I might hit a wrong note. I might accidentally turn two pages instead of one and you'll hear a wonky couple of measures until I get back on. *I am human and sight-reading can be challenging.* No matter how tempting it is, do not shoot me a "whiplash glance" when this happens. This just makes you look bad. If later you don't get the callback, and it makes you feel better to tell yourself that it was all my fault, go for it.

> **Tip 6:** After your song, make sure to say "thank you" to me as you leave the room.

After the audition, think about how it went. If I didn't play something like you wanted me to, don't immediately jump to the conclusion that I am just a bad accompanist. Show your music to another pianist and ask them why they think the audition might have gone poorly. If you find it helpful, record your audition with a voice memo app on your phone so you can analyze it later. Did nerves get the better of you and you rushed through rests without realizing it? Did you think you told me something at the piano beforehand but you totally forgot? Did you skip a couple of bars? *Look at each audition as a valuable learning experience* and save the "I had a horrible accompanist" excuse as a last resort.

Best of luck with your next audition! Maybe I'll see you there.

Chapter Takeaway

The Keys to a Successful Start

The audition room can be a daunting place, especially if you are not as familiar with how it works. And those extra nerves as you walk into the unknown can affect you in all the wrong ways, especially your voice. Here are a few reminders to help you prepare as much as possible so you can ease into the room like a pro.

- Smile as you walk in the door.
- Acknowledge the table, briefly, but head with confidence directly to the accompanist.
- Have your clean audition cuts ready at the front of your binder:
  - Organize the rest of your book with only songs you are confident singing, ones that will show the auditors something different than your audition cuts.
  - Take out everything else—no need for excess clutter.
- Practice speaking to the accompanist—if you don't have a piano player handy, ask someone from your team to just listen to what you will say. They can at least help you slow down and be clear about what you need for each song.
- Speak calmly and kindly to the accompanist, and ensure that you two are on the same page with both songs.
- Head to the center of the room, not too close to the table—the auditors want to see all of you.
- Smile again at the table and pause. If they are still writing, you can say hello again.
  - Remember, you wrote down your audition songs so there is no need to officially slate. When you say hello, you can say your first name to ensure that they are looking at the correct audition form and materials.
- There is no need to rush these first moments. Take a deep breath and look back at the accompanist, then go for it!

10 | "From the Top—5, 6, 7, 8"
THE DANCE CALL

WITH SEAN MCKNIGHT

I am drawn to people who are comfortable in their bodies and excited to learn about storytelling through dance. I'm also drawn to people who, instead of saying "I can't do that," say "I can't wait to do that!" Also, in a way that a lot of auditioning students might not expect, I very much notice what people are doing when they're not dancing, but observing their peers—I like people who are contributing to a positive and supportive atmosphere. Mostly, I want to make the students who don't have a lot of dance training feel comfortable, and to help those students that do have a lot ascend to the next level.

—Michelle Chassé, Professor, Musical Theater Dance, and Director, Musical Theater Dance Intensive, Boston Conservatory at Berklee

F OR MANY APPLICANTS, THE DANCE call is often the most dreaded part of the audition process. You've undoubtedly spent weeks—if not months—rehearsing your songs and coaching your monologues to the point where they feel like old friends. For many of you, the uncertainty of what to expect can cast a shadow of doubt and fear on your confidence. *What if it's too hard? What if it's too easy? What if I can't pick it up fast enough? What if I've never taken a dance class?* Rest assured: no matter your background or skill level, it's only natural to be nervous. As you walk into the studio, take pride in who you are, and embrace what is special about you. You are your own secret weapon.

Dance Call Basics

- My first goal is to put everyone at ease. Walking into a studio with a professor and three student assistants can be intimidating. Take a *deep breath* and *relax*. A roomful of nervous energy can be a breeding ground for anxiety. Harnessed adrenaline, however, can be a great tool. It's much easier to be yourself when not surrounded by strangers. Therefore I begin each call with a round of introductions—yours. We are about to spend ninety minutes together where my number one goal is getting to know you. What better way to start than by asking your name and hometown? It's amazing how something this simple can have such a positive effect. Everyone suddenly feels more approachable and the room isn't so formal.

- Remember, this audition is my chance to not only *gauge your current level of dance*, but it also serves as a time for me to see *how well we would work together*. I'm most interested in seeing your learning process. Though I will eventually be evaluating how you perform the combination, much of my critique will come from me *watching you learn*.

- There's no way to get around this: the combinations will be hard but also short—between eight and twelve sets of eight. (For those of you new to dance, an eight is two measures of four in music.) To best gauge your ability, I deliberately teach combinations that are challenging. This isn't meant to intimidate. It's essential that I give dancers their moment to shine, but not at the expense of everyone else in the room. I intentionally choreograph a *realistic audition dance that you would encounter in the professional world*. It will be demanding, but it will also be rewarding and actor-driven.

- The dances will change from year to year but the structure will stay the same. I'll always start with a peppy musical theater combo that gets the blood going. It will be fast-paced, character-driven, and will most likely include a mix of sharp movements, clean lines, and quick directional changes. The second piece will be a ballet based dance choreographed to specifically contrast with the first. It will be a very fluid combo designed to showcase long lines, controlled turns, and a variety of leaps. It's short, sweet, and to the point.

- If tap is your thing, don't worry—you will have a chance to shine after the other two combos. I'll ask for you to show me your favorite time step and then an eight count of double pullbacks.

Learning the Combinations and Dancing in Small Groups

The only thing that is a negative for me in a dance call are people who seem to be trying to prove their dance training, flexibility, or technique to the room. We will see all of that—we don't need you to do a triple when the music and choreographer dictated a double, for instance. Just trust that your technique is under you and with you always—you don't have to continually prove anything.

—John Simpkins, Head of Musical Theatre, Penn State University

- We will spend the bulk of our time together learning the musical theater combination—usually forty-five minutes. I break the dance down into phrases of eight and program your body step-by-step, stacking the phrases on top of each other until we reach the final pose. I'm a big proponent of muscle memory. Just in case you have a resurgence of nerves, we will program your muscles to execute the movement even if your brain is trying to play tricks on you. Lines will rotate frequently to make sure everyone can see; I don't let anyone hide. And questions are always welcome, as is going back and breaking something down again. I want you to be confident when you dance in your small groups and that often involves going over problem sections more than once. *If you are struggling with a particular phrase, there's a good chance you are not alone. Don't be afraid to speak up.*
- Once everyone is feeling more confident I add another layer—acting. *The motivation behind the movement is just as important as the step itself.* Acting is the through-line in musical theater and must translate into your dance. If you are having a hard time grasping a step, understanding why you are doing the movement can help with your ability to execute. Don't underestimate the value your acting plays in the quality of your dance. If your goal is to be a Broadway performer, then it is vital to you that you be capable of not only completing the movement but also telling the story. I tell people all the time, if I start looking at your feet, you are doing something wrong.
- After about thirty minutes we break the room down into three or four groups to give you some more space. At this time I will also stop dancing and allow my student assistants to take the lead so I can watch. This is when things will really start to pull together. Each group will dance three to four times, and in between each round, I'll give individual corrections and answer any questions that arise.

Remember, corrections are a good thing and should be viewed as positive feedback, not criticism. If I'm able to isolate one or two moments within your dancing and ask for you to make an adjustment, it means that you are doing something right.

- The final groups of four are a necessary evil, but please don't self-sabotage! You will be tempted to put an undue amount of pressure on this moment, but remember, this is not the only time I will see you perform the combo. This audition tends to be very interactive and by this point, I will already be familiar with you and what you bring to the table. *Don't let nerves creep in.* The final small groups are an opportunity for me to be reminded of you and your talent, and they provide me the chance to write down my thoughts and observations from the entire course of the audition. I want you to succeed. I will even have the student assistants dance with you on the side.

- After you dance I might ask you some questions about your training, your special skills, and maybe even your involvement with sports—it depends on what I see from your performance or read on your résumé. Sometimes I will give corrections and have you do the combination again, and sometimes just one time through is all I need. Do not read into this; there is no method to my madness here. I don't get another callback so I take my time to be sure that I have all of the information I need.

Tips for Dancing in Small Groups

- While waiting for your group of four, stand quietly on the side. *Never sit.* You should also refrain from dancing along. Review the combination in your head as you watch other groups go. Remain calm and take a deep breath.

> **Tip 1:** If you feel yourself starting to panic, take a deep breath in through your nose and exhale twice as long through your mouth. Works like a charm!

- Pay attention to the placement order—such as first dancer downstage right, second dancer upstage, third dancer down, fourth up.
- Maintain your spacing while you dance. Stay in your window.

- When you have finished dancing return to your starting position until you are once again dismissed to the sides of the room. Try not to look out of breath.

At auditions I always ask for advanced skills (gymnastic, multiple turns, tap)—ADVANCED—and often what I see is not. I feel that some auditioning students feel they need to show moves, any moves, thinking if they don't, they will not be accepted. This is not true. Don't show your weaknesses. When showing special skills, they must be truly exceptional.

—Robin Lewis, Associate Professor for Musical Theatre/Dance,

Rider University

Our time together will go quickly. When it's all over I truly hope that you will leave the studio with a strong sense of accomplishment. *I also hope that you have fun.* You are Broadway's future and I am thrilled that I get the chance to spend a few hours with you before the rest of the world knows your name.

Amy here! The dance call is often one of the most anxiety-producing aspects of the audition process. Even more so than the song and monologue portions, each program has different requirements for dance, and no two movement auditions will be the same. But I wanted to reassure you that no matter how the call is structured, each school and adjudicator is looking for the same thing in potential students—an actor who can move, someone who listens and takes corrections, and, most importantly, a willingness to try. We all really do want you to succeed to the best of your abilities:

Sell whatever you have and commit to it. It doesn't matter if you get it wrong, it matters that you try your best. I will say, seeing a student give up on the storytelling, even if they don't have the technique, can really hurt them. Students can learn technique—that is what school is for—and our dance call is really designed to simply identify which level of class a student would be put in, beginning, intermediate, or advanced. It's not to rule people out, simply to evaluate their ability level. Students who quit on the floor and don't at least try can be a red flag.

Breathe and trust that you are meant to be there. Don't assume your lack of dance training is going to knock you out. We take all different levels of dancers, movers, and nonmovers. Try to have fun and show us who you are.

It is an opportunity for us to learn about your personality and attitude as well as your dance ability.

—Kaitlin Hopkins, Head of Musical Theatre, Texas State University

If you are not a dancer, do not be intimidated by the dancers with more training. Just do what you do. You may be viewed as an actor who has the capacity to be trained and as someone who can tell a story with their movement.

—Mark Madama, Associate Professor of Musical Theatre, University of Michigan

Presence in the room draws my eye immediately. Of course, I love seeing beautiful technique on a dancer, but when someone comes in with excitement, confidence, and their passion, and they are giving "I want this," my eye goes right to them.

—Robin Lewis, Associate Professor for Musical Theatre/Dance, Rider University

Advice for the Nondancer

Remember, we really are on your side, no matter your skill level!

- *Show that you are willing to learn, and try your best. It never hurts to smile and have a sense of humor.*
- *Remember: it is about the story. Connect the movement to a character or a narrative. So much of what we strive for in musical theater dance is about using movement to advance a plot; even the smallest or simplest-seeming steps and movements can embody so much about a given character or intention.*
- *"GO FOR IT! Don't apologize—no matter how much or how little technique or training you may (or may not) have. I always remember the people who have the most positive attitudes and who absolutely do not apologize, in words or in body language, for what they're attempting."*

—Michelle Chassé, Professor, Musical Theater Dance, and Director, Musical Theater Dance Intensive, Boston Conservatory at Berklee

- *Don't give up—keep trying to get the right steps, the right arms.*
- *If you consider yourself a "nondancer," then let the singer and actor in you take over: get musical and storytelling clues from the music and choreography and commit fully to that.*

- *"Hold your spacing so you don't crash into others around you. Be aware."*

—Tracey Moore, Professor, The Hartt School, Theatre Division,

University of Hartford

- *You are going to be in the room with others who have different levels of dance skills. Do not compare yourself, and know that the next four years in your college training is to make you more skillful and confident in dance.*
- *Come to the dance call as an actor first. Like the saying goes, Passion can't be taught, but I can teach you the steps.*
- *"Give yourself a 'pat on the back' for something positive you did or learned from the experience."*

—Robin Lewis, Associate Professor for Musical Theatre/Dance,

Rider University

Chapter Takeaway

Dance Call 101

- ### Do not apologize for your dance abilities.

Be proud of who you are. Everyone is unique and brings something special with them to the room. It's not a crime if you aren't a trained dancer. Don't beat yourself up for not spending your entire childhood taking jazz, ballet, and tap. A lot of what I look for is *potential*. I'm not casting you as an immediate replacement in a show, I am assessing your current level, and where I feel you can progress over the course of the next four years.

- ### Dress the part.

Don't think that because you are about to get sweaty that it is okay to be sloppy. Show your body off to its best potential. Present yourself in a polished, professional manner.

- Bring all of your shoes: tap, ballet, jazz, and heels/characters. You never know what is going to be thrown your way and you will want to be prepared.
- Ladies: Unless specified, your hair doesn't need to be up in a bun, but long hair should be pulled back from the face. If you are wearing a leotard and tights, remember that the line of your leg will look longest if you wear shoes the same color as your tights. Unless we are doing a ballet combo, ditch the ballet skirt.
- Gentlemen: Avoid basketball shorts. They cut off your body line and will greatly affect your ability to do combinations that require knee work or slides. Pants (athletic, jazz, or a dress pant of stretch fabric) and a form-fitting shirt are your best bet for audition attire.

- ### Be a mimic.

Make yourself look just like the choreographer. Pay attention to all of the details and pick up the nuances. I guarantee you that it will be noticed.

- ### Try.

A little goes a long way. Dive in and give it your all. Resistance and insecurity can be viewed as attitude and get you labeled as difficult.

- This is your party.

A top Broadway casting director visited my school while I was in college. He offered a piece of advice that has stuck with me throughout my entire career. He said to say to yourself, "This is my party," before you walk into any audition. It's true. This is your party. We are all here to see you and we want you to be the one.

Be pleasant. Be patient. Be kind. And show that you have passion for every aspect of theater!
> —Michelle Chassé, Professor, Musical Theater Dance, and Director, Musical Theater Dance Intensive, Boston Conservatory at Berklee

11 | "The Room Where It Happens"
THE DAY OF

We want you to have a good experience. I have no investment in scaring you,
proving how good my school is, or putting you down in order to lift me up.
I want to meet you and get to know you briefly. So, do whatever you need to get
comfortable in front of strangers. Start early enough to be secure. But, please
don't over-rehearse the piece. Instead, practice investing in the relationship with
your imaginary partner, committing to the goal of the character in the moment,
and living freely within that.
　　—Joe Deer, Chair, Department of Theatre, Dance, and Motion Pictures, and
　　　　　Director of the Musical Theatre Initiative, Wright State University

THIS CHAPTER IS FULL OF important information because this is it,
the day. I've provided many guidelines, tips and tricks, and advice
from as many of my colleagues as possible to help you navigate
this day from waking up to the final exhale of relief once you've finished.
Read through everything carefully, and even go back and reread sections
as you create your game plan for making this a successful day.

On-Campus Auditions

Each school will run their on-campus auditions slightly differently, but
they will all share basic similarities. Regardless of what school you
are auditioning for, the following four components will be assessed in
some way:

- **Singing:** Often two 32-bar cuts or one minute each of contrasting
  material.

- **Acting:** Often two contrasting monologues.
- **Dance:** Often assessing ballet, jazz/theater dance, and tap skills.
- **Interview:** This may be as formal as sitting in a chair across a desk or as informal as being asked a question after you do your monologue.

Packing Checklist

- ☐ Address of audition location and other school-related documents
- ☐ Five headshots/résumés
- ☐ "Book" of music
- ☐ Audition outfit
- ☐ Audition jewelry
- ☐ Audition shoes
- ☐ Dance call outfit
- ☐ Dance shoes (find out what you need to bring)
- ☐ Copy of your monologue(s) for your reference
- ☐ Personal steamer—one for your clothes if needed and one for your voice
- ☐ Audition journal
- ☐ Water bottle
- ☐ Recorded tracks and something to play them on (for Unifieds)
- ☐ Leave your perfume at home!
- ☐ Snacks

What to Wear

You will need two different outfits for your audition: your dance call outfit, and your singing/acting outfit. (For examples of what to wear during the dance call, see that section at the end of this chapter.)

Remember that everything you do in this process teaches us about you. What you wear can help with that. You can give us glimmers into who you really are from what you wear. Style, point of view, confidence, and your awareness of what is appropriate are all very telling. Here are some guidelines:

- Dress like you really, really care.
- Dress like this is one of the most important days of your life.
- Dress in a way that makes you feel spectacular and grounded.
- Dress in a way that won't restrict your movement. The shorter the dress or the tighter the pants, the harder it likely will be for you to feel free and connected to your body.

- Dress in a shape that flatters you. Embrace your body. Find something that fits your body's shape. Don't hide—embrace. You are exactly who you are, and that is wonderful. Be your best you, and don't try to be anything else.
- Dress in a color that flatters you. And patterns are fine too: just make sure they are not too overwhelming or distracting.
- Find fabrics that don't wrinkle. You will be traveling a lot and you don't want to be ironing your clothes if you don't have to.
- Stylish jewelry can be a great addition: just make sure it doesn't get in your way.
- Wear shoes you can confidently move in. Heels are fine if you can move freely and truly be grounded in them. Don't wear one-inch character shoes . . . **ever**. Wear real shoes in your singing/acting audition.
- Bring an extra audition outfit. You never know how you will be feeling the day of your audition and having another option can help ensure you feel the most confident about yourself in that moment.
- Make sure your dresses or skirts are not too short. Ask someone you don't know their opinion of the length. If they hesitate, then it is too short.
- Yes, you can wear jeans if they are nice and not ripped.
- Ladies—yes, you can wear pants and no you don't have to wear hose or tights (unless you want to).
- Finally, you don't need to wear a scarf to be an actor. Take the scarf (and the jean jacket for that matter) off.

For many students, this decision is often one of the most anxiety-producing choices during this process. You want to look good, but also look like yourself, not like someone going to a job interview or church. To ease your mind and give you a little insight into how we feel about "audition wear," and if and when it impacts our decisions, I asked my colleagues to say a few words:

> Audition outfits can be an immediate representation of who you are as a person since this our first introduction to you. I would recommend you wear what you feel makes you the happiest. From the moment you walk into the room there isn't anything that happens that doesn't in some way influence the impression you will leave. This is part of the overused and hard-to-explain expression of "be yourself." Do not try to second-guess what the auditioners are going to want you to be wearing. That being said, a

well-groomed applicant who gives the impression of wanting their auditions to go well and would like serious consideration is always something you want to think about when choosing your attire.

—Mark Madama, Associate Professor of Musical Theatre,
University of Michigan

The audition outfit is important, but not a deal breaker. I prefer that students wear something representative of who they are in everyday life. If you are edgy, go ahead and dress edgy. What I don't like is when students wear clothes that do not allow them to move freely, and the worst is when the student cannot walk comfortably and naturally in their shoes.

—Matt Edwards, Associate Professor and Coordinator
of Musical Theatre Voice, Shenandoah University

I wish actors would think a little bit more about clothing that they look good in AND feel comfortable in. The only time an audition outfit influences our decision is if the actor appears uncomfortable, tense, or self-conscious about what they are wearing. The actor needs to be able to move, sit, stand, et cetera, comfortably, without having to worry about their clothing.

—Tracey Moore, Professor, The Hartt School,
Theatre Division, University of Hartford

Sometimes, actors wear clothes that completely contradict the material. If you're singing a Golden Age song cut, or doing a monologue from Our Town, *you probably shouldn't be in a miniskirt and heels. If the character is high-status, you shouldn't be wearing jeans and tennis shoes. So many actresses do the Viola ring speech from* Twelfth Night *in a dress. Pay attention to the given circumstances and work out a plan for what you wear that reflects your choices, without being a costume. It's like a blind date: you want to make a good impression, but most importantly, be yourself. On some level, it doesn't matter what you wear, and on some level it does matter. Find the right balance and be comfortable so that you can do your best.*

—Catherine Weidner, Chair, Department of Theatre Arts, Ithaca College

Best advice . . . rehearse in your outfit, especially the shoes you're going to wear! Your outfit is an opportunity to feel like you on a great day (not you dressed up to go to church or a cocktail party) but something that is simple and can reflect all the different characters you are going to show us. For

134 | The Ultimate Musical Theater College Audition guide *example, if you are in a fancy dress and heels, and the character in your monologue is a runaway or a kid from a small town, or perhaps you are singing a song from* Rent *or* Next to Normal, *your outfit choice might be better if you have on a nice pair of jeans and a blouse, and maybe boots, not heels. That choice would suit your material better. Ladies, you don't have to wear a dress. Pants, slacks, and nice jeans are also great options.*

—Kaitlin Hopkins, Head of Musical Theatre, Texas State University

The photos here are a few examples of good audition outfits. This is just to give you an idea of where to start. Remember, we want to see *your* personality, and there are countless ways you can achieve that.

Day-of Etiquette

It is important to remember that we are mining for clues about you from the minute you start your application. Because we often have only five minutes in the audition room with you (sometimes less, sometimes more), we need to gather all the information we can to make our decision. Even if it doesn't look like it, we are watching everything you do. From the minute you walk in the door, someone from the program will always have an eye out. That is not meant to scare you, but to empower you. Here is what we are looking for.

- How You Talk to the People in Charge

You want to be your fun, open, and charming self during these auditions, but sometimes anxiety can translate into abruptness or rudeness without you even knowing. Basically, no matter what, be kind to everyone who is helping with the auditions. This includes not only the faculty and staff, but also the student assistants and guides. When asking questions, be concise and make sure that you are able to be relaxed enough to listen to the answers. It can be very telling if you were just given an instruction to change into your dance clothes and then you turn around and ask when you are supposed to change into your dance clothes.

- How You Interact with Your Fellow Auditioners

We know this is a stressful time, but one thing that might help is to remember that you will be auditioning with other students who have

PHOTO 11.1–11.3 Here are three examples of great audition outfits for women. Ladies, you do not need to wear a jewel-tone dress and nude heels (unless you feel great in that look). Be colorful, be bold, but show off you! Photo 1 – black top, red/black/white skirt. Photo 2 – all black. Photo 3 – white top, orange pants.

PHOTO 11.4–11.6 These three photos are just the beginning for great audition wear for men. Show us your personality with color and patterns. And, remember, you don't have to wear a collared shirt if that is not you. Photo 4 – white shirt, black pants. Photo 5 – pink sweater, gray pants. Photo 6 – blue and white shirt, black jeans.

the exact same goals as you and are as just as nervous. Your job is not to make friends (though that is bound to happen), not to be a hero (someone lost their dance shoes, you give them yours, and now you are shoeless), and it is definitely not to judge (what anyone is wearing, singing, etc.). Your job is to be friendly, open, and focused. You may be auditioning with friends or you may not know anyone, but, regardless, you have to remember that this is game day; this is go-time. You are here to do one thing only—to present yourself as the best possible you. Be kind, be generous, but also be a little bit selfish; this is your time to shine.

• Volume

We all know MTs can be very LOUD, but in this situation especially, it can be interpreted as immature or anxious behavior. Check yourself and make sure you are harnessing that extra energy in a strategic way.

PHOTO 11.7–11.9 You truly have so many options for what to wear. Don't be afraid to mix it up, depending on your song choices, the different programs you are auditioning for, and how you feel that day. All three of these work well, but each one has its own twist. Photo 7 – black outfit, bright, patterned scarf. Photo 8 – red and black dress. Photo 9 – black jumper with colorful shoes.

- What You Wear

See above.

- What Repertoire You Choose

Refer back to chapter 4.

- How You Talk to the Accompanist

Refer back to chapter 9.

- How You Handle Yourself in the Room

The room can be stressful, we understand, but we want to meet the real you when you walk through the door, not the overly amped or too-controlled version of you. Find some way to ground yourself in the space. Be careful not to go on autopilot during your audition, as you will just go through the motions and forget to listen. You want to be able to read the room enough to get a sense of what is happening beyond you, yet stay in the moment. This is a tricky balance. For example, if you walk to the center of the room and slate your two songs after we have said, "Hello, how is your day?," it can be telling. Enter the room with a sense of gratitude and ease. You can be assertive, sure, but not aggressive. Speak up so we can hear you, look us in the eyes when you talk to us, and do your very best not to push your energy too hard. Don't forget, we already like you, you did pass the prescreen after all!

> *As a faculty member, I am trying to evaluate your potential and figure if our program is the right fit to help you reach that potential. I look for an applicant's artistic abilities and aesthetic, teachability, openness, and a sense of genuine inquiry. Don't try to "blow us out of the water"—bring your best self and your complete skill set into the room. Be ready to take adjustments and discuss your training and goals.*
>
> —Jason Debord, Assistant Professor of Music, Department of Musical Theatre,
> University of Michigan

- How You Introduce Yourself, or Your "Slate"

A "slate" can be defined as the introduction of your audition pieces. This can come in a variety of ways, so you should ask the monitor (the person sitting outside the door to help with the audition flow) if the auditors want you to slate or not. This will take away the mystery and possible awkward-ness of that first minute in the room. Many times we will have your song/monologue choices written down on a form you filled out, so a slate may not be necessary. But there may be times when the auditors will ask for a more formal slate. In high school (for competitions or auditions), you may have been taught to slate by saying, "Hello, my name is X, I am X years old and from X. I will be singing X with music by X and lyrics X from X, followed by . . ." This is much more than we need. Try, "Good morning, everyone, this is X followed by X." That is really enough. But just like everything, each program will be different, so simply ask. We can learn about your warmth, generosity, excitement, focus, and ability to adjust to the energy of the room through your slate!

- What Your Headshot and Résumé Look Like

See appendix B for materials that will help, as well as a résumé template.

- How You Manage Your Energy

You need to be on your best professional behavior for your auditions, and this applies to your space and energy as well. Those who choose to major in Musical Theater are typically very high-energy and outgoing. The balance of staying friendly and open but still making sure you are in "game-day mode" is a really, really tricky thing to master. If you are waiting to go into the room to do your monologues and someone tries to talk to you, you can simply say, "I don't mean to be rude, but I really need to have a few quiet moments before I go in the room. Can we finish this conversation when we are both done?" Or you can simply put your headphones on (whether you are listening to anything or not) to block out the noise. If you are extra loud and hyper in the holding room, looking through other people's books and singing and twirling, then we will notice (or be told about it after). There's a good chance that your focus in the audition room will be all over the place as well.

Things We Love (and Don't Love) to See in the Room

But what, you may be asking, are we *really* looking for in an audition? If I could answer that in a single sentence, or paragraph even, I wouldn't need to write this book. Everything in this business is subjective and one person's idea of the perfect audition will not be the same as someone else's, even if they are sitting behind the same table. However, there are qualities of great auditions (and bad ones) that are pretty universal. I wanted to present a few opinions on what makes a successful audition so you can see where personal preference and general ideas overlap to find a good balance in your own audition. After that, I compiled a list of behaviors and actions that we all (my colleagues from around the country) find "off-putting" in the audition room.

What We Love to See

- *An actor connecting with the musical introduction before they sing.*
- *Discovering the text instead of reciting meaningless words.*
- *"Making specific, personal choices—taking risks."*
  —Victoria Bussert, Director of Music Theatre, Baldwin Wallace University

- *Healthy, free singing that is connected to breath and impulse.*
- *A sense of immediacy in why they need to communicate.*
- *"A connection to the person to whom they are singing—the 'other' or 'opponent' in the scene."*
  —John Simpkins, Head of Musical Theatre, Penn State University

- *A clear story presented truthfully—no excessive gesturing or "acting."*
- *A student who knows the kind of roles they will play and has done the work to find something that highlights them appropriately.*
- *"I love to see students put their best foot forward. If they don't belt, I don't want them to try. The same goes for singing legit."*

—Matt Edwards, Associate Professor and Coordinator of

Musical Theatre Voice, Shenandoah University

- *Restraint and finesse—they are so* RARELY *trusted in an audition. There is no need to rattle the rafters or redefine "forte."*
- *Solid musicianship—pitch, line, musical values, character-true singing, and so on.*
- *"Thorough, realized acting values."*

—Hank Stratton, Assistant Professor, Acting/Musical Theater Division,

University of Arizona

- *The student actor knows what they do well and brings at least that to the table.*
- *Authenticity—doing the pieces from the student's point of view, not the way it "should" be done. That doesn't mean to ignore tradition, but live comfortably in the song.*
- *"The student is well rehearsed, but not over-rehearsed."*

—Joe Deer, Chair, Department of Theatre, Dance, and Motion Pictures,

and Director of the Musical Theatre Initiative, Wright State University

- *I love to see the "Light." I cannot explain this light. Denee Benton had it. Corey Cott had it. Megan Hilty had it. Kyle Beltran had it (on and on). Who cared that their voices were not perfect at their auditions? Not me. There was a light shining from their eyes that attracts and moves the listener. There was also a vibration of love combined with a touch of nerves and a willingness to share their world with me, a total stranger. I was truly moved by their vulnerability.*
- *I love to see a smile. Seriously, a genuine smile when talking and exchanging pleasantries. Most students are so frightened they simply shut themselves down and lock their true selves into a "slating and singing machine." They have left their warmth and personal charisma in the hallway.*
- *"I adore when the singer can find the new thoughts in the text as though they were discovering them for the first time. This change of thought is always accompanied with a change of focus. The eyes move as the thought*

changes instead of staring straight ahead in a zombie-like state at the same spot. Wow, now is that impressive!"

—Gary Kline, Assistant Option Coordinator of Acting/Musical Theater,
Teaching Professor, Carnegie Mellon University

What We Find Off-Putting in the Room

Amy here! When I asked my colleagues what they felt did not work in the audition room, many responses overlapped or were very similar. To avoid repetition, and to help you understand that these behaviors are things that no one likes to see in any room, I am combining them into one helpful list and keeping them anonymous.

- *Applicants who aren't fully prepared. Mistakes are inevitable and forgivable, but not being prepared is something in your control and therefore irresponsible.*
- *An unprepared student who does not bring a picture and résumé and is not "on top" of their audition monologues.*
- *An actor who comes into the room with their "want/objective" to be liked.*
- *Someone who is defensive and has a negative attitude.*
- *Every single moment is completely planned. Some applicants are all set with a slate that's planned, and when they walk in the room, we might say, "Good morning, what are you going to sing for us today?" only to have the actor begin to blurt out their rehearsed slate as if we hadn't just spoken to them. Relax and be a person.*
- *When I feel like I'm being spoken to the way the auditioning student thinks I want to be spoken to. I don't want to be told what they think I want to hear. I want to encounter them for real, as young humans with thoughts, fears, and opinions of their own.*
- *I do not want my personal space at the table invaded by someone singing too closely to me or moving up to the table as they sing. I call it the "creep" because they creep up closer and closer as they sing. I once had a young lady crawl to me and try to sit on my lap! I also hate being stared at so that I feel I must engage with the singer.*
- *Pay attention to the size of the room and calibrate the volume of your singing (especially if you're belting). We're right there, usually five to six feet away from you.*
- *LOUD does not equal ADMISSION.*
- *I am disappointed when, if given a direction to make a different choice, the actor/singer does not have the ability (or is not willing) to transform and adapt.*

- *When I get the impression that I am being shown the full and complete breadth of talent in one small audition. There is not time to sing every style you can, dance every step you can, and show every range of emotion in a monologue. There IS, however, a chance to do good, simple, specific, and truthful work. Trust that that is enough!*
- *When someone isn't able to be "present" in the room. Usually this is nerves and fear that prevents someone from "being in the room." I usually ask people to take a breath, look around and take in the actual room, and then start their work.*
- *Students who mistreat a monitor or pianist. (We will find out.)*
- *When we ask if the student has any questions, and they ask us something that (a) we already covered in the information session, which shows they weren't listening or (b) isn't going to be helpful to them in making a decision about college, such as "what do you think is the future of acting?" That's a missed opportunity for you to learn about our program, and a waste of time for us to try and answer.*
- *I dislike the need for "approval" or feedback. An audition is not a class and I am not there to teach.*

The Morning of Your Audition

Wake up early. Eat a good breakfast and plan to bring snacks with you. This can be hard to do when you travel, so plan ahead. Chances are you will be staying in a hotel, so do what you need to do to get a good night's sleep. If you can work out or do yoga before your audition, that might help to get your energy flowing. Lay out your clothes the night before. Pack your bag the night before. Have a checklist so you don't need to have someone run back to the hotel to find your tap shoes or favorite lipstick (see the checklist above). Make sure you are staying super hydrated as travel and hotels can really dry you out. Bring a personal steamer or other tools that you know will warm your voice up.

It is also a good idea to talk to the team member that is bringing you to the audition about how you want them to handle the experience. Do you want to be dropped off? Do you want them to go on a tour of the school? Do you want them to wait with you for support? When it is over, do you want some quiet time to reflect and not talk to them? Do you want them to ask how it went? Discuss this ahead of time, and if you are a member of the "team" reading this book, then I think it is a good idea for you to lead that discussion. I know your instinct is to be with them at every step, but they might not need or want that. Be mindful of this component because you want to do all you can to support them and they might not have the vocabulary or heart to be honest upfront. Follow their lead.

An Audition at Pace University

I thought it might be helpful to take you through a typical on-campus audition. Here is a sample on-campus audition schedule:

> **Tip 1:** Remember, all schools will do this differently, but knowing what to expect at one place may give you an idea of what to expect at others.

When you are initially granted your live audition, you will be given one of two audition slots—morning (9:00 am) or afternoon (1:00 pm). For this example, let's assume that you were given a morning slot and were put into group A.

8:00–8:30

Arrive at the audition site and check in. There will be a large holding room with a check-in desk and space for you to wait, stretch, and change. You will be assigned a group, which will determine if you will dance first (group A), sing first (group B), or do your monologue first (group C).

8:30

Let's say that you are dancing first, so you will immediately go and change into your dance clothes. Make sure you know what shoes you need to bring with you into the room, but most programs will assess you in jazz, ballet, and tap. If you are not a trained dancer, just bring a pair of shoes that you can move well in. There is no need to buy new tap shoes if you have never tapped before. Once you are in your clothes, start stretching!!

> **Tip 2:** It is not appropriate for you to do the dance call in your singing/monologue outfit. The dance component requires different clothes for obvious reasons. Even if you have never been in a dance call or class in your whole life, you still need to dress for this audition. See chapter 10 for more details.

8:50

All groups will be introduced to the audition faculty and their audition leader who is a current student and you will be brought to your respective audition (singing, dancing, acting). This is where you separate from your "team" member. This is a great opportunity for that person to take a tour of the university, go get coffee, meet other team members, or talk to the program representatives.

9:00

Because you are in group A for this example, you will be brought into the dance audition space and given a number to pin to yourself.

9:00–10:15—Dance Call

You will most likely be taught a ballet combination and a Jazz/Musical Theater style combination. You will be given time to learn and perfect the moves, then you will do the combination in groups of three or 4 at a time for the auditors. This audition will typically have current student assistants in the room, so really lean on them to help you learn the dance or style. Not everyone is a dancer and we don't expect you to be. We do want to see how you handle the call, though. This is often more important to us than how well you can dance.

10:15–10:30

Change from your dance clothes into your singing/acting outfit. During this time, you should also be warming up your voice (see tips on that below). Grab your "book" and get in line for your singing audition. Don't forget your water bottle, focus, and breathe. This is not a time to chat; this is a time to prepare and get ready.

10:30—Waiting

You will be put in an order to go in and sing. Sometimes there are chairs to sit on, sometimes there won't be. Sometimes you will be able to hear people singing, so focus is key. Use your headphones if you need to block the "noise" out. The monitor (usually the student who is leading you) will give you instructions about what the auditors want you to do as soon as you enter the room. If you have any questions about that, just ask; the current students are there to help you!

Take a big inhale. On the exhale, enter the room with a sense of grounded joy.

> **Tip 3:** My biggest piece of advice is that you must take your time in the room. You will probably not be in there for more than five minutes, and while your instinct will be to rush to get everything in, the reality is that you need to take every single second. This is YOUR time. This doesn't mean doddle or go slow, but you do not have to rush . . . at all. We are on your side, I promise. We want you to be the one, so if you are rushed, it can put you on autopilot and we will not be able to truly "meet" you.

Enter the Room

As soon as you enter the room, do your best to make eye contact with the auditors. It is appropriate to say something like "Good morning" or "Hi everyone" as you enter the space, but know you may or may not get a response back. More often than not, they will tell you what to do, but if they don't, the first thing you should do is head to the piano. *Tip: The accompanist is going to be your biggest ally in the room.* Often, the auditors will not be done writing or talking about the previous person, so the best place for you to wait is at the piano. This is also a great time to talk the accompanist through your songs (see chapter 9 for an in-depth explanation of *how* to talk with your accompanist). Take your lead from the auditors, but once you can sense everyone is ready (or are told that they are) . . .

Head to the Middle of the Room

Sometimes there is an X or other mark on the floor, but often it is up to you to find the strongest spot in the space. Usually, that spot is about seven feet back from the auditor's table. Once you find it, make a connection with your auditors before jumping right into your songs. This can be your slate, but it can also be a moment to show a little bit of your personality, the real you. Then you sing. There is always a chance that we will ask for additional material or make an adjustment on something you presented and have you do it again. This is a great opportunity to see how you work on your feet and what you do when you are thrown "off." Make sure that your book of music is very organized because if we ask for something else, you need to know how to find it right away!

11:15(ish)

Once you are done singing, you will be moved to the monologue room.

> **Tip 4:** Some schools will have you do your songs and monologue together in the same room.

You will enter the room one at a time as you did to sing, and head to the center of the space. You will introduce your piece(s). After you do, take a moment to collect yourself before you begin. No more than fifteen seconds are needed for this prep. There will be a chair to use if you wish. When you are done, you will often have a brief conversation with the auditor about why you chose the material you did or what your dream roles are. When that is complete, say thank you and leave.

12:00

You are done. Take a few minutes to write in your audition journal about your experience. Include what you sang, who you met, how you felt. Then BREATHE and find a way to let the day go. Maybe take a tour of the university or dorms (if this is available). Walk around the campus. Eat in the cafeteria. Plan lunch with a current student. Go get tea with some of the new friends you met. The key for this audition—and any other audition you will do in your life—is for you to know that now that it is done, you have absolutely no control anymore. None. You must find a way to let it go. Sing with me . . . "LET IT GO . . ."

What about the Interview?

This most often takes place in one of the audition rooms and typically comes in the form of a casual discussion. You may be asked about why you picked your repertoire, what your dream role is, or why you want to study in New York City.

The Dance Call

For most programs, the dance call is considered a placement audition more than a make-or-break part of the incoming audition. In fact, I have found more and more that if dance is not a priority of the program, they may not have any dance call as part of the initial auditions, especially at Unifieds. This is great news, as dancing is often the most terrifying component of the day because it is very much out of your control—simply put, you have no idea what they will throw at you.

The most important thing for you to think about is staying focused and present. There is so much that we are learning from you during this time, and the best thing you can do for yourself is to be open to whatever we might ask of you and to just go for it. We are looking to see how you pick up direction, how you behave in the room, and, yes, we care about skill and technique, but we are mostly looking for what kind of actor you are through dance. If you consider yourself a "dancer," then this will be another opportunity to show your personality and skills, but be wary of taking that too far. If the space is small or the room full of people, large tricks and turns will just seem out of place and dangerous. The dance auditors will be able to see your skills in their combinations, especially when they give more challenging options. If you have a spectacular trick, save it for the small groups when there is more space and you can really shine in a safe and controlled way.

Each school will run their dance audition differently, but typically, the dance call will have a ballet combination and a jazz or Musical Theater style component. Most programs will tell you what to wear and what shoes to bring, so be prepared for what you already know how to do. If you have never taken a tap class before, don't buy a new pair of tap shoes, but if you own jazz shoes, bring them.

What to Wear

Dressing for the dance call is often just as hard as picking your song and monologue audition outfit, especially if you are not a dancer or not used to being in a dance studio. But the best part is, it doesn't matter what you wear, as long as you follow a few simple guidelines:

- Wear tight or form-fitting clothing that allows you to move freely and gives the auditors a chance to see how your body moves. This usually means a mix of cotton and spandex (or some other stretchy fabric).
- Do not wear baggy sweatshirts or sweatpants. You will get lost in all that bulk, it might impede your ability, and the auditors will not be able to see your movements.
- Women, you don't need to wear a leotard and tights, unless that is what you feel most comfortable in. Yoga pants, spandex shorts, tank tops, and tighter t-shirts are also acceptable.

PHOTO 11.10–11.13 As with the other auditionwear photos, this is just to give you an idea of where to start. Remember to find clothing that moves well, makes you feel comfortable, and shows a little personality. You will have plenty of other things to think about in the dance call: what you are wearing should not be one of them. Photo 10 – red leotard, black skirt. Photo 11 – All black leotard and leggings. Photo 12 – blue tank, black pants. Photo 13 – gray shirt, black pants.

- Men, you don't need to wear dance tights or spandex pants. Form-fitting running or sport warm-up pants (as long as they aren't too baggy) or stretchy dress pants work well. Also, make sure your t-shirt or tank top is tighter as well.
- Make sure you try moving in your outfit before you get to the dance call. If anything pulls funny or restricts your movement or feels uncomfortable, find something else.
- Think about showing a little personality here too. Wear your favorite color or find a fun pattern. This will help you feel more comfortable in the dance call.

For a more in-depth look at the dance call and what to expect in the room, see chapter 10.

How to Warm Up Your Voice (Anywhere) before Your Audition

Advice from Voice Teacher, Andrew Byrne

Singers should think of warming up their voices in the same way that athletes prep for the big game. In the sports world, players do stretches, strength work, mobility exercises, and mental focus drills to make sure they are ready to play safely and effectively. A singer's approach to warming up for an audition should involve these same concepts, and you can't expect to do your best work if your voice and body are not primed for action. The challenge comes when the realities of the college audition world present themselves: often, there is no practice room provided for you, and singing full voice in the hallway outside the audition room is not the best idea. So, short of commandeering a bathroom stall for your scales and arpeggios, what can you do before your appointment time to get your voice in the zone? Here are four ideas to try.

- Mouth the Words of Your Song

If you mouth the words of your song in rhythm, you will be warming up your articulators (jaw, tongue, lips). Additionally, several postural muscles of your larynx will be moving and getting warm, even though your vocal cords will still not be touching. Try it out; touch your larynx (Adam's apple) with your fingers as you mouth the words to a song, and you'll probably feel some movement there, even though you're making no sound.

- Sing while Covering Your Mouth

If you completely cover your mouth, you can sing a song with your full voice without much actual sound leaving. This is the principle behind the Belt Box (beltyafaceoff.com), which is a mask-shaped product that covers your nose and mouth to muffle sound waves. If you don't want to spring for a Belt Box, you can use your hand to cover your nose and mouth to get much of the same effect.

- Sing on "Ng"

If you say the word "sing" and go right to the last consonant, you'll be able to feel the position I'm talking about. The tip your tongue will be on your lower front teeth, and the body of your tongue will be on the roof of your mouth. You can sing your melody like this, and the sound will again be coming out of your nose. The advantage of "ng" is that you can use the front part of your tongue to articulate the words of your song, while still leaving the rest of your tongue on the "ng." It sounds a bit funny, like an alien language, but it helps to focus your airstream and makes singing feel easier. If this sounds confusing, I demo this technique on my site (andrewbyrnestudio.com).

- Sing Your Song through a Straw

Before your audition, stop by the food establishment of your choice and grab a drinking straw. Seal your lips around one end of the straw, and sing your song through it. Singing in this way creates what's known as a "semi-occluded vocal tract." This is a fancy way of saying that the tube of your throat is narrowed and lengthened. In addition to making the sound quieter, this technique helps your vocal cords meet more efficiently and lets you warm up quicker.

Chapter Takeaway

Frequently Asked Questions

- ### Can I start my song or monologue again?

Only if it's truly necessary. If you blank on your words or, for some reason, start in a different key than your music is written, start over. But if you can save it—do.

- ### What if the accompanist is playing the song at a tempo that doesn't feel like how I rehearsed?

See chapter 9 for more information about this, but if it is truly not going as you anticipated and there is not a way to recover, then, yes, you can stop. But you can really only do this once and you must not ever blame the pianist. You can say something like, "I am so very sorry, but I must not have given the tempo I intended. Would it be possible for me to begin again?"

- ### What if I forget my music?

Always carry a digital backup so, if need be, you can have the pianist play it from an iPad or other device. You can also talk to your monitor and see if they can help you find the sheet music in the program's library.

- ### What if I am sick or injured prior to my audition date?

Get in touch with the recruitment coordinator of the school and talk about what to do. Accommodations can be made if possible. Perhaps it means bringing footage of you dancing if you are injured. However, if you are physically unable to sing, it makes no sense for you to make the trip to audition. For some schools, it may mean a lost audition, but for others, they will do their best to accommodate you at another date. This will vary school by school.

- ### What if the person before me does the same song or monologue?

Frankly, I would try to think of this as a positive. It will absolutely not matter on our end, so why should it matter on yours? Plus, no one will do it like you—so embrace that opportunity!

- ### What if the people around me are really annoying?

Block them out any way you can. Wear headphones, focus on your material, or you can even say, "I would love to chat, but can we wait until after the audition?"

- Can I start my song or monologue on the floor?

Definitely not for your songs, but it is a possibility for your monologue if you HAVE to—and chances are you don't have to.

- Can I bring a recording?

You may only sing with a recording if you are auditioning at a location where the school does not provide a pianist.

- Can I sing a cappella?

No.

- Do I have to memorize my monologue?

Yes.

- Can I take my shoes off?

Only if you really, really have to because of what you are doing with your material. But honestly, if you have to, you should probably plan to wear different shoes.

- Can I request feedback so I know how I did?

No. We get asked this all the time and while I wish this would be something we can provide, it is simply not possible. We see too many people to be able to provide this to everyone, so please don't ask or expect this.

- What if they ask me to do something that I am not comfortable with?

This depends on what is being asked of you. If they ask you to belt and you don't or never have, you can say something like, "I have never done that before, but I am willing to give it a try," versus saying something like, "I don't belt. My voice teacher told me it would ruin my voice so, no." This second response isn't helpful because it shuts you down to possibility or to us seeing something in you that you had no idea was there. Try to say yes to what is being asked of you.

- My monologue or song has a "bad word" in it. Can I still use it?

Yes. If you are uncomfortable with the language or content of the material, don't choose that material. And be mindful as to where you are too, as some schools will be sensitive to this and others will not. Personally, I don't think a monologue with explicit and extensive profanity is the first impression you want to give us, so keep that in mind when you are selecting material.

- What if they cut me off?

It usually means they have seen what they needed. Don't take it personally.

- Do I shake hands with the auditor when I walk in the room?

Not unless the auditor initiates it. We tend to audition during cold and flu season, and many prefer not to shake hands during that time.

- What if they give me an adjustment in the room? Does it mean I did something wrong?

An adjustment is when you are asked to do your piece over again with a certain correction or different perspective in mind. Many times it is helpful to see how you take direction and how well you listen and synthesize what is being asked of you. When this happens, stay open to the suggestion and have fun. This is a great opportunity for you to be able to show them more, so use it!!

- Where do I look when I sing or do my monologue?

Not at the auditors. Unless you are specifically instructed to. Otherwise, you need to find a spot that is just above and behind our shoulders. No need to fixate on that spot, but that is where you want to establish the person you are speaking to. Also, no, you do not need to put an empty chair in the space to "pretend" that they are sitting in it. We know where you are focusing and why.

12 | "Something's Coming"
MAKING THE DECISION (ACCEPTANCES)

Remember your joy—no one is ever forced to pursue a degree in Musical Theater.
—Victoria Bussert, Director of Music Theatre,
Baldwin Wallace University

Thank You Notes

Before we get into the main event, I want to discuss *thank you notes* for a minute. This topic is also very subjective, but I will say that while I love the sentiment of a thank you note, the reality is that we get FLOODED with them. So much so that the effort (and time . . . think of all the time) that is spent handwriting them tends to go to waste because of the sheer volume we receive. My recommendation is that if you want to write some kind of thank you—and, no, it does not give you a leg up—write a very brief thank you email that has a personal anecdote from your audition. The key here is that you *absolutely should include a photo of you* in the email. Here is an example of an actual thank you letter that I think makes a good template.

Dear XXX,
I had a wonderful time auditioning for your program on February 15th. I felt at ease the entire time and especially found the students running the audition so helpful. Thanks for commenting on how you liked my song choices of "It Might as Well Be Spring" and "Never Fall in Love with an Elf"—I really like them too. I felt at home at your school and it is my great hope to be a part of your next class.

Wishing you all the best,
XXX

Acceptances

It is important to remember that an acceptance to the university is not the same thing as an acceptance into the performing arts program. At this point in the process, you will know if the university has accepted you or not—often you must be accepted to even audition in the first place. If you have not received an acceptance to the university yet, then please call the registrar's office. Most programs can't give you your audition results unless you have been accepted to the university itself.

Now you are just waiting for your audition results. If you are admitted into a program, you will receive a formal letter with your acceptance and more often than not a personal phone call. If a school makes calls, then that will typically come before the hard-copy letter arrives.

The Letter

- This can come as regular snail mail or in a digital form. Read it very carefully and save it in a safe place. Make sure you note all the pertinent information, including all deadlines, the on-campus student days, and any other important dates. This letter also includes all *decision and deposit deadlines*, which are very important to keep track of, especially if the dates vary with each program. The lines of communication with you and the program will now be open, and you will have many opportunities to ask any questions to help make an informed decision. We want you to feel free to communicate. We want YOU and so will other schools, so don't be surprised if there is a lot of communication on our end. The polite thing to do is always respond as swiftly as you can.

The Phone Call

- Many programs that accept you will call and tell you directly. Typically, this call will be from the director of the program or someone in recruitment. Giving the good news is one of the best "jobs" I have in my position. I wait all year for the moment I tell a prospective student they are accepted; it is pure happiness.
- This call can be overwhelming. If you pick up, make sure you are in a safe place to manage your excitement (not driving, for example), and are able to write down important information. Sometimes it's better

to let the call go to voice mail so you can have a record of the moment and then go back and listen again for the details.

- We can't (at least I know I can't) make all the acceptance phone calls in one day, so if you hear that others are getting "the call" and you haven't, don't fret. Notifying everyone can take a week or so, and patience is the name of the game.

- If you don't receive a call, that doesn't necessarily mean you didn't get a spot. It could mean that you are on the alternate list, the wait list, or perhaps we are waiting on additional information. However, no phone call could also mean that you have not received a spot. And no matter how agonizing the wait is, please don't call the program. This is our busiest time of the year, and you will get an answer in some direction soon, but calling to ask your status is in bad form. (*For more on wait lists and what to do if you are not accepted, see chapter 13.*)

Tip 1: Make sure that the phone number on ALL your forms is the same. Many times, there will be a different number on your résumé than on your prescreen submission or university forms. We need to know where to call and while I would welcome talking to a parent on the home phone number that was on our form, I would prefer to be talking directly to you.

Tip 2: Make sure your voice mail is set up and that your mailbox is not full. You would be surprised how many people I call where I can't leave a message.

Tip 3: Breathe, listen, and be present on the call. We don't expect you to give an immediate answer, but be prepared for questions like "Have you heard from any other schools yet?" or "Do you need me to connect you to housing or financial aid?" Be polite and joyful, and regardless of how you feel, do not tell any school they are not your first choice.

Tip 4: By now, you will have a more specific idea of what kind of program you want to be in, and in many cases, your acceptances have narrowed down your decision considerably. You should also have your financial aid package and scholarship information from the university, which will be a crucial part of the final decision. Use these tools and gut feelings to help guide you through this process, and remember that this is about the best-fit school for you.

Tip 5: If you know you won't be attending a school that has accepted you, then you need to put that in an email to the program director or recruitment office as soon as possible. I am going to say this a lot in this chapter . . . because I really mean it.

After the Call

- The call will be followed up with a formal letter or email (depending on the school) with information about financial aid, scholarships, and accepted student day events and details.
- This is all happening between March 15th and May 1st, the final deposit day nationwide. Students have every right to wait until May 1st, though you will find pressure from the programs to make a decision as soon as possible so we can manage our wait lists.
- **As SOON as you know you are NOT going to accept a particular offer, you really must tell that program.** *I cannot emphasize to you how important this is.* (Yes, this is bold for a reason.) Remember those stats from the beginning of the book about how many hopefuls audition for each program each year? As you know by now, we only have a certain number of slots and so very many people who want them. We implore you: for the sake of anyone on the alternate list/wait list/priority wait list (each school calls it something different), please tell us you will not be accepting the offer so we can move on. It is absolutely within your right to wait until May 1st, but if you know at any point before, then please do the respectful thing and tell the program.
- If you DON'T know whether you will accept an offer, then make sure you communicate that as well. In addition to the initial acceptance phone call or letter, there will be plenty of opportunities to communicate with the head of the program or recruitment. We will be reaching out to you on a consistent basis to find out where you are in your decision-making process and what we can do to help you make your choice. Get those questions ready so you can collect all the information you need to feel comfortable with your decision.
- We want to help you. We want you to be honest with us. We want you to come to our school/program and will do whatever we can

to make that happen. This means that you need to do your part by communicating with us. Reply to emails, return phone calls, let us know what other programs you are considering. I would also recommend that it is you (the student) who does this, not an adult team member. To the team: you can call financial aid, housing, and ask other logistical questions about attending the school, but the communication with the program head or recruitment should be from the student if at all possible.

- This is also a good time to utilize social media. Start friending or following those students you met at the audition from each of your accepted schools. Ask them questions from a student's perspective and see how they describe the program, the classes, and the university life. I find this is a great chance to get the "insider scoop." They will be honest with you (or at least we hope they will), and they can also connect you with alumni or to anyone else who might have another perspective you'd like to hear.

- The recruitment process itself should also be a deciding factor for you to determine the right fit. Do you like how the university/program is communicating with you? Do you feel comfortable with the correspondence? Are you feeling unnecessary pressure from a particular school to make a decision? Do they make you feel special and wanted and give you the space you need to factor in all the details? This can be telling about the program as much as about this process, so check in with your comfort level when you need to.

Accepted Student Days

If it is possible, I strongly urge you to visit the colleges that accept you. There is no substitute for your "gut feelings" about the faculty, the students, and the campus, which you can only get from visiting.

—Tracey Moore, Professor, The Hartt School, Theatre Division,
University of Hartford

There is no way for me to emphasize more strongly that you should do your very, very best to attend the Accepted Student Day for each of your top programs if at all possible. By now, you should have a narrowed-down list and if you are lucky enough to get accepted to multiple programs, then we are talking about visiting only two or three schools. Typically, these are overnight events where you stay with current majors in the dorms, eat in the cafeteria, sit in on classes, attend university-wide events, and hopefully see a performance as well.

There are also events planned for parents/family/team members where they can meet with housing and financial aid. I know (*I know*) how incredibly costly this can be—especially on such short notice—but I have found this to be the most effective way to make your final decision. *My advice is to budget for this prior to the auditions, knowing that it is an essential part of the process.* Many teams will ask why they need to do this if they are auditioning on campus. My response to that is, when you are auditioning, you are not in the mindset of being a student. You are in audition mode. And as mentioned before, there is programming on the Accepted Student Days that isn't offered on the audition day.

These Accepted Student Days are even more essential if you auditioned at one of the Unified auditions because you will not have seen the campus yet. I almost guarantee that if you attend one of these days, you will know where you want to accept. You learn SO much from being a student for a day: you see the program's teaching style in person. You see the students, the faculty, the performing arts facilities, and the dorms. You feel the energy of the environment, and most importantly, you can determine if you actually SEE yourself there as a freshman. This is an invaluable investment to make as it can ensure that you are making the right choice for you.

Once you have made the best decision for you and your family, then send an email to the head of the program (or whoever you have been communicating with) and say in that email that you are accepting the offer and when you plan to deposit. Also, YAY!!!!!!!

The Money

For me, this is the hardest part of the process simply because we (the program) have very little control over it. Some programs will have scholarships, some will not. Some universities will offer great financial aid and some will not. Hopefully, you will have been working on getting scholarship money on your own, and your guidance counselors are helping you and your family so that no matter what you are given by the university or the program, you have some kind of cushion to make your choice possible.

If you have not received a financial aid package that is going to work for you, then appeal it immediately. I have seen great success by doing this. Typically, it means sending an email or making an appointment with the financial aid office to talk about options, and they will give you the info you need to appeal the decision.

As far as talent scholarships go, you can always ask the program if they have any and what you would need to do to be considered for them. Full-ride scholarships are really a thing of the past. Very few programs are able to offer them and even partial university scholarships are hard to find. *Don't bank on being the recipient of one of these.* You may be the most talented student that your high school has ever graduated, but so is everyone else who got in. There are numerous professionals who help deal with finding outside scholarships, and their resources and experience can be worth the cost of their services. I recommend that you start looking for as many ways to fund your education as possible right now.

Outside Scholarships

I have a student who has fully funded her Musical Theater education through outside scholarships. She is not an expert at this, just a really resourceful and driven student who knew that the only way she could attend the program of her dreams was to figure out how to pay for it on her own. And she did. I asked her to give me, and you, some tips on where to start and what to focus on when applying in order to give you the best chance of financial success.

Zoe's Scholarship 101

A scholarship organization or individual will consider an applicant based on their essay, academic record, and other interests and involvement. Each component is important in its own way. Here are a few tips and things to think about as you apply.

- The Essay

Your scholarship essay should describe who you are and why you need the scholarship, regardless of what the topic is.

- Utilize the topic wisely to incorporate important details about yourself. For example, if you cannot afford college because your single mother works three jobs and has two other children to look after, in an essay about your aspirations, consider discussing how you would eventually want to provide for her. Use provocative language. Paint a picture. Invite the reader into your community.

- Be careful of rambling or going off-topic.
- A scholarship essay should be expository, narrative, and persuasive.
- It should form a relationship with the reader.
- Do not boast. No one wants to give money to someone who is entitled or doesn't seem to care. Instead, figure out ways to celebrate, cherish, showcase, and illustrate both your accomplishments and your financial needs.
- Be warm.
- A base essay can be recycled and reused.

- Academics

Standardized test scores and your GPA will factor into a funder's decision.

- To help with your SAT/ACT scores, utilize a prep coach if it is available to you. If not, seek out test prep books from the book store or library and create your own "class."
- Take the tests as many times as you can. If you can't afford the fees, ask your guidance counselor if a fee waiver is available to you. Often, those who qualify for free or reduced lunches or similar programs will also be able to have the fees waived.
- Your GPA, or your "being good at school" measurement, is up to you. Show up to class on time, be prepared and organized, stay focused, and study. This will help your grades be the best they can be.
- Be careful not to overload yourself with AP classes or extracurriculars your senior year. Preparing for college is a big deal, and you need to give yourself enough time to prepare.
- And, remember, GPA and test scores do not determine your intelligence.

- Involvement

Community service and extracurricular activities are important, but don't feel like you need to be involved in or volunteer for everything.

- In the community, find a cause or organization that really speaks to you and your beliefs. I volunteered for Equality FL, a group that advocates for gay rights at festivals.
- For clubs and school functions, sometimes less is also more. Instead of being a member of many groups, try being a leader of one. This can be more impressive on scholarship applications too.

- Think Local

When searching for scholarships, ask your guidance counselor for local businesses and organizations that offer money to students. Also look to your county and city websites for more opportunities.

- Other organizations can be women's clubs, arts societies, community foundations, country clubs, 4H, and so on.

- Form Relationships

If you receive a scholarship, the first step is to send a genuine thank you card. Then reach out to the person or organization with updates periodically. They will be happy to know where their money is going and to see that it is truly benefiting you. This will especially help if the scholarship is one you have to reapply for every year.

Tip 6: Parents, please, please, PLEASE be honest and realistic with your kids about what your family can afford. Decide what debt you are willing to take on prior to the audition process, and figure out your max financial capacity. If they know this going in, it will help "soften the blow" if they can't go to their first choice because of resources. Be realistic and have a plan, but please have a plan. I can't tell you the amount of dreams I see thwarted because families go into this with a "we will figure it out" point of view. You may not figure it out and your child may only be able to afford one semester. It is devastating to watch.

The Deposit

The university deposit to claim your spot in a program is not a great deal of money (in the grand scheme of things), but it is a very important final component in the process. The deposit is the official signal to the program that you plan on attending in the fall. It will often secure your place in housing as well. Each university will have a different deposit amount, some only $100. You may have accepted your spot on the phone, or even made a post about it on social media, but I always wait for the deposit notification as the official word that you will become a part of the incoming class. Once you deposit, consider your audition season officially over.

Social Media

- It is in your best interest to *not* post anything official about this process on social media at all. Nothing about where you got in, the scholarships you have, or what auditions you liked or didn't like. We don't want to learn from social media that you have made a decision and you did not let us know first. In fact, you really should not be posting about official information at all. It is not professional or in good taste. Once you have made your decision, informed all schools waiting to hear an answer, and everything is squared away, then, sure, flood people's feeds. Before then, it's just not cool.
- You will probably be asked to join Facebook groups, both formal and informal, for the programs you audition for by students or the faculty/recruitment team. My advice is to hold off on doing any of that until you have made your final decision. It can give the school a false sense of acceptance and become confusing for the other decided students in the group. If we have not heard from you at all, we may go looking on social media to see if you have posted anything, but don't make us do that. Just be honest and upfront with each program in a timely manner.
- There may also be Facebook groups for your team to join so they can be connected with this process. There are great communities of parents, teachers, and mentors affiliated with each school. I know many parents of alumni that are still connected to each other because of the community they found during the audition process for their kid.
- When you have made your decision and put in your deposit, this is our signal that you are IN. Now is the time to join all the groups and start connecting with those who are also accepted. The Accepted Student Days are also great for creating these connections because you will meet a good number of your future classmates. This is also a great opportunity to begin looking for roommates and building a community within the program.

Your Gut

Wherever you end up, you are going to be just fine. Most theatre programs share the same goal: to make you the best theatre artist you can be. Each program does it a little differently so don't get caught up in the quantity. Pay attention to the attributes of each program, and audition for the ones that make sense for YOU.

—Catherine Weidner, Chair, Department of Theatre Arts, Ithaca College

Over and over I have seen young students, even as young as twelve, say that they dream of going to a particular school someday. They have their "dream school" merch, and they obsessively follow what the school does on YouTube or Instagram, but once they see the school in person, they really don't like it. Something doesn't feel quite right and their gut tells them it isn't the right fit. Then there is the program that is new and relatively unknown, they auditioned for it because of a random recommendation, and they got in, visited the school, and LOVED IT. Is it worth going to your dream school that maybe won't live up to your dream expectations? Or is it better to go to the more unknown school that gives you the impression you will thrive there and fully enjoy your time? You just never know. But my advice is to go with your gut and not with the name—just because it is a name. Incredible talent comes out of every program, and while it is true that name recognition can be valuable, it certainly should not be *the* deciding factor.

I do firmly believe that in this difficult process, you ultimately end up at a school where you belong. Not everyone can get into their dream school but that doesn't mean all is lost. It only means the dream is just beginning at another place that will hopefully nourish and challenge your artistic and creative spirit. There is much to learn from the audition process, and it might not always be what you hoped to learn, but go into it with your eyes and heart wide open.

—Grant Kretchik, Associate Director of the School of Performing Arts,
Director of BFA Acting, Pace University

"SOMETHING'S COMING" | **165**

Chapter Takeaway

Picking the (Personally) Perfect Program

Your audition season went great. You were prepared with great songs and monologues that showcased your particular talents and personality, you entered every room relaxed and with confidence because you knew what to expect on the other side of the door, and you did your best and had fun no matter how hard the dance combination was. And now you have the difficult and wonderful task of narrowing down your top school choices to only one. Here are a few tips to help you decide:

- Think back to your auditions. How did it feel to be at each school? How were the faculty and students?
- If you can afford it, attend the Accepted Student Day on campus. This can give you an even better idea of what it's like to be a student in that program and is invaluable if you did not audition on campus.
- How are your conversations with the faculty and recruitment staff? Do they answer all of your questions? Are they excited to have you join their program?
- How does money factor into your decision? Which program gave you the best financial aid offer or scholarship opportunities? If the best offer didn't come from your dream school, can they match it?
- If the program is well established, how are their alumni doing in the "real world"?
- If it's a young program, does it offer something new and exciting that really speaks to the kind of training you desire?
- When you think about your life in the fall, where do you picture yourself?
- What does your gut say?

In the end, you'll be happiest if you pick the right fit for you.

13 | "Whatever Happens, Let's Begin"
WAIT LISTS AND REJECTIONS

Trust that your life has a purpose, and listen to what the universe is telling you as you receive your letters of rejection or acceptance. You are being guided toward what your purpose is in life, and I truly believe pursuing acting, singing, and dance is a calling to change the world through your musical gifts. Not everyone is cut out for this life, no matter how much you loved the art form in high school.

Do not believe your self-worth hinges on the results of your auditions. *You will continue to be special and unique, no matter how you make your living. Success can simply be defined as being happy. So pursue what makes you happy in your life!*

—Gary Kline, Assistant Option Coordinator of Acting/Musical Theater,
Teaching Professor, Carnegie Mellon University

WHAT HAPPENS IF YOU ARE one of the many students each year who don't get accepted into any BFA programs? Or what if you are one of the many who are accepted to places you are really not interested in going? It can be heartbreaking. So much effort, energy, and money is spent during this process, and this unexpected outcome can be just devastating for you and your support team. There is often a true mourning period where you question your abilities and dread a future full of the unknown. The one thing I can tell you for sure is that while it may feel like the end of the word, it is most certainly not. Somehow you need to trust me on this. It is only one of many stumbling blocks you will experience if you go forward with a career in the performing arts.

There could be a million different reasons that you were not accepted and, unfortunately, you will never know why. In this situation, calling or emailing for feedback is not appropriate: the amount of people auditioning is so high, there is no conceivable way we could give feedback to everyone. In fact, most schools will have a policy of no feedback. This can sometimes leave you feeling unresolved and I often hear people say that if they knew what didn't work, they would change it. Your team, coaches, and teachers will need to help you work through this time and these feelings. And, remember, if you are going into this business no matter what, then rejection will become a part of your life. You learn to accept it and move on. This might sound cold, but it is real.

We get endless phone calls and emails from parents/team members who beg us to reconsider, reevaluate, or reexamine the results. This typically comes from those who were accepted to the university itself with good financial aid or scholarship offers. These calls are really tough—for both sides—because there is literally nothing we can do once the decision is made. The compassionate part within us all wants to help, but once that decision is made, it is final. Calling to tell us that you were cast as Eponine in your spring musical, that you just won a competition, or that you were accepted to other programs won't change our minds.

> **Tip 1:** According to her very informal poll, Mary Anna Dennard, a college audition coach, says, "If a girl auditions for 14 schools she will get into 2.5 of those schools. The .5 being a wait list or deferral."

Program Responses

It is almost guaranteed that you will be rejected at some point during this process, and I think it is very important to talk about how you want to handle it with your team. Each school will give their results differently—some will send a letter and some you can access online. Have a plan in place so you can be in control of how you receive the information and prepare yourself for any outcome. Do you want to be the person to open the letter or do you want a team member to do it for you? My advice is complete transparency, but everyone is different.

You will receive one of four possible answers to your audition. Every school will use different terminology, which can be confusing, so make sure you read everything you receive from the school carefully, and call if you have questions. Two words that will be consistent will be "accepted" and "rejected." What can be confusing is what is in the middle. The following definitions might help.

- Accepted

You are offered a spot in a program you auditioned for. *See chapter 12.*

- Alternate or Priority Wait List

This means that if someone from the first offer list doesn't accept, then that spot would go to the next person on the alternate or priority wait list. Programs create these lists in many different ways. Some might do this based on type or gender to keep the class balanced.

- Wait List

If you are put on the general wait list, it means that offers have been made to the first round of admitted students and if any of them do not accept, the program will go to the wait lists and offer admission AFTER they go through the alternate or priority wait list. Each school will handle this differently. Again, some will go to the wait lists in a certain order, some will base the offers on type or gender, and some will be arbitrary.

- Rejected

You are not accepted into the program and were not put on any alternate list or wait list.

> **Tip 2:** Some schools will have an alternate/priority wait list AND a general wait list. Basically it means that offers go out to everyone on the alternate/priority wait list before they go to the general wait list. Other schools will only have three categories: accepted, wait list, or rejected.

You Are Placed on the Alternate List/Wait List (Alt/WL)

If you are an Alt/WL, there are a few things you can do to let the school or program know you are still really interested:

- Email the head of the program to say that their school is your first choice and, if accepted, you will immediately deposit (if that is possible).
- Check in every few weeks. It is important not to bother the admission staff or program head too often, but a quick email can be a helpful reminder.

Alt/WL Waiting Game

It is possible that you get put on the Alt/WL for your top school and get into some of your second choices. What now? This is when it gets tricky. You could be on that list until the end of the summer. There is always the possibility that if someone drops out for whatever reason they will go to you. However, I would use May 1st as the day when you release the possibility of getting off that list and move on to your next choice. This is when going to the Accepted Student Days of the schools you *did* get into is really important. It will help you decide which of your second-choice schools might be a good fit.

Your instinct may be to call the school and ask where you stand on the Alt/WL, but many won't tell you because most spots are not "numbered" like that. You can ask how many others are on the list and see if that helps to sort your plan out, but again it probably won't. Somehow you need to trust that it will work out and you will end up where you need to be.

Wait List Specific Details

This is how Pace University's recruitment director, Wayne Petro, explains wait lists:

A wait-list result can happen at either the academic or performing arts level:

- *Academically, a wait-list decision means that your admission is dependent on a number of factors—perhaps your grades or test scores are below the admission criteria but not low enough that the college is willing to deny you. Rather, they are pausing your record until they determine how their initial offer letters yield deposits, or how many admitted students commit to attending in the fall. This can be a tricky position for a performing arts applicant that also needs to begin or complete the audition process. For a school that requires you to be academically admitted before auditioning or before they admit you, this delay in being academically admitted could be detrimental to meeting commitment and deposit deadlines. If you are in this position, I recommend remaining in close contact with both the admissions office and the performing arts personnel who manage your application.*
- *Being wait-listed for the performing arts program also means that your artistic admission is paused until the department assesses its ability to accept you. The timeline for this varies per school.*

The family who finds itself on a college's wait list—either academically or artistically—would do best to do all the advance research to know if the school is the right fit financially and personally. Basically, lead with the careful assumption that the wait list will turn into an offer. It may not, but at least if it does you are in a position to quickly put down your tuition deposit and secure your spot in the program.

Parents and students on the wait list often ask me if they should deposit elsewhere in the event we don't end up admitting them. My answer is always a careful one: only deposit to a school where you truly expect to go; however, if you choose to put down a "safety" deposit, make sure you know the deposit refund deadline so you are not out a few hundred dollars should your first-choice school end up granting an admission offer.

Moving Forward

I turn away talented hopefuls every year; maybe I've even turned away "the next Meryl." If this is what you want to do, keep going, no matter what. Do not let any single audition or admission decision take away your dreams. Fight for what you love and go towards it, but remember, if there is doubt in your mind, it is worth examining. I was once a good candidate trying to get into good schools just like you. It's humbling now, sitting on the other side of the table holding future dreams in my hand. I want you to know that no matter the outcome, simply getting up, preparing, and putting yourself out there in the audition makes you brave, strong, and truly admirable. It will serve you no matter where life takes you.

—Grant Kretchik, Associate Director of the School of Performing Arts, Director of
BFA Acting, Pace University

Once the sadness subsides, turn that energy into fuel and work to figure out the next step. Start by talking about it with your team. There is no right or single way to handle this: it is very personal. So here are a few ideas of what you can do if you know you want to re-audition.

• Hire a Coach/Change Teachers

If you have done the audition season without a coach, I would recommend trying this route. It can be a very good investment, especially at this stage. If you had a coach the first time, you may want to change your voice teacher or acting teacher. This is not a time to worry about the feelings of those teachers that have been with you for a while. They need to understand that something didn't work and that you need a new ear/eye.

- Take a Gap Year

For many, a gap year can be a gift. If you view it as a positive experience, then you can really make use of the time in a productive and effective way. Maybe you need more work on your singing, acting, or dance skills. Maybe you need to modify your college list, or your song and monologue choices, or get your grades up, or make money. This time gives you a chance to do that. A gap year is also a great time to travel and gain new life experiences. Or it can be your chance to work and save money for college or the next step you choose. I find that those who take a gap year are often more ready to learn than students who come directly from high school. It really doesn't matter to us if you take a gap year or not, but to you it can make all the difference. Be sure to give this time structure and direction so you continue to work toward your goals whether they are applying for college programs again or something new.

- Should I Go to the University Anyway?

You get a big scholarship to the school of your dreams but you don't get into the program, so what do you do? If you choose to attend a university without getting into the program, you need to know that re-auditioning the following year and getting accepted into the program is very rare. You shouldn't expect to be accepted into the program just because you are already attending the school. It is a big gamble, one that can lead to even more disappointment, and one that I wouldn't take. On the flip side, if you know you want to re-audition, then there is something to be said about getting some "core credits" out of the way. My candid advice is that if you choose to go with the plan to re-audition you must be aware that your chances of getting in after a second audition are very, very small. There are many reasons for this:

- If you go to a university where you are not actively training, then your skills will lag behind considerably. You must be studying as intensively as you were in high school, if not more, if you expect to compete with the next incoming class. It is often hard for a nonmajor to get voice, dance, and acting training, so you would need to actively seek this outside of the university. This can come at quite a cost, and that must be factored in.

- Socially it can be challenging. It is most likely that you will have been friends with like-minded people all through high school, performing, training, and socializing with people who do what you love. If you go to a university where you are not in the major with the people who are doing what you love, it can often feel isolating and you might be envious of those who are talking about theater all day, every day. For some it is fine, but I have seen many who chose this path and then have a hard time finding their place.
- The other thing that makes this choice difficult is that it puts SO MUCH pressure on that single re-audition for the program. All your eggs are in this one basket and if you are not super ready, the pressure can be insurmountable. You need to have a serious backup plan if you don't get in. I recommend that if you re-audition for the program of the university you already attend, you should also plan to audition elsewhere. I also recommend that you have a plan if you don't get in. Do you stay at the university? Do you consider changing paths? You don't need to know right away, but try to stay as realistic as you can.

- Community College or Another University

You may want to consider a community college or a university close to home. This will allow you to knock off a few core academic credits and give structure and a purpose to your time. You will also want this school to be close to a place where you can train and study your craft so you can up your skills and audition technique. Just know that when you re-audition the following year, most programs will see you as a freshman in the program even though you have credits. Regardless, this can be a good way to keep your school momentum progressing toward your ultimate degree.

- I Got into a Program That I Don't Love. Do I Go Anyway?

This is SO personal. I believe that you can learn something no matter where you go if you are open and ready to receive it. If you have the recourse and many of the other components feel right, then there are many reasons to consider going. I would not go thinking that you are going to re-audition for other programs and transfer out (though that may be your plan). I would go in with the mindset that you are going to learn all you can and get everything you possibly can out of it. Who knows, it may turn out to be the school of your dreams. On the flip side, this is an incredible amount of money to spend on something that may not be right for you.

- Nondegree Granting Program or Move to New York or Los Angeles

There are many nondegree granting programs that offer great training. These are typically two-year programs in New York City or Los Angeles. Some will offer housing, but many don't. You could consider moving to a big city and setting up your own "postsecondary" training, but this choice requires a lot of courage, maturity, and resources. This would include living on your own; taking voice, dance, and acting classes; and, essentially, making your own program. I tend to not advise this for anyone right out of high school, but some individuals are ready for the challenge. Exploring a year of this could teach you a lot about yourself and will definitely help you determine if you still want to pursue a college education.

Gap Year Testimonials

I think a gap year can be an incredible opportunity to breathe, regroup, grow up, self-evaluate, train, make money, and travel. Below are three accounts of students who have taken a gap year.

Nate

Taking a gap year may have been the best decision of my life.

For most of my high school career, I was very interested in math and science: specifically architecture and engineering, which led to physics and the "hard" sciences. I was all set to pursue physics when I graduated as well, having been accepted to several schools with good physics programs. However, during my sophomore year I threw a wrench into the whole thing and caught the acting bug.

I had been convinced by a friend to take drama class to fulfill a certain arts credit, and she promised it would be an easy A. What I didn't expect was to thoroughly enjoy the class and come back the following year, despite having already fulfilled all my arts credits. That next year I learned I could sing. With no experience or belief in my abilities, I got up and sang "Happy Birthday" for my class and it was good.

As you can see, there was a big conflict within myself. I was completely invested in the sciences and applied almost exclusively to schools with good math and physics programs, with little regard for much else, especially the arts. I thought theater was great but just a hobby. But when

I entered the Beach Blanket Babylon Scholarship for the Arts contest and became a final vocalist, I realized that I could actually pursue theater and singing outside of high school.

With my applications for physics already submitted, I was too late to audition for theater programs and I decided to take a gap year. This year would give me time to prepare and also to travel, something I've always wanted to do. I moved to Australia in September after graduation and over those four months away, I filmed and submitted my prescreen video (a logistical nightmare) and also took acting, voice, and dance classes to keep up my training.

I am very thankful for the time I spent abroad; it helped me mature and gave me experience in the "real world," lessons that helped me thrive in college.

After I got back from Australia, I worked and saved to fund my travel to the in-person auditions at the LA and Chicago Unifieds, as well as to pay for a vocal coach to help with audition prep.

In short, I used my gap year to reevaluate my goals and move my desired major from physics to Musical Theater. I also used the opportunity to travel and further develop my experience and skills as a performer. The year off allowed me to focus on college auditions and to figure out what I truly wanted to do with my life.

Hillary

I didn't want to settle.

When I didn't get into my top schools for Musical Theater, and I did not want to settle, I decided to take a gap year. I wanted to get my money's worth. Affording college is no easy feat, and if I was going to pay a ton anyway, it had to be for a top-notch program.

I was scared and embarrassed, but it turned out to be the best decision ever! I did a show with a youth theater company called "Kidz Theater," and landed a manager and an agent. I took dance classes consistently, booked some TV and commercial jobs, and kept working a 9–5 day job. I got a taste of the "real world" and really understood that Musical Theater was exactly what I was meant to pursue.

When I got into my top choice, I took college very seriously. Now that I have had sufficient training, I am ready to take on this career path. And I already know exactly what to expect after graduation day!

Ryan

My auditions went so well, I was relieved it all happened the way it did, one year later.

In the winter of 2013 I was preparing for the New York City Unified auditions when I found out I could no longer attend because my family was financially incapable of getting me there, let alone pay for college. This came as a shock; I thought my family was doing all right. But it turns out we were still suffering extreme losses from the housing crisis of 2008, as my dad was a high-level real estate manager. This made my senior year extremely difficult to complete because I now had little incentive to finish my education: I wasn't going to college like all the rest of my friends and I wouldn't be pursuing my dream career either. I became the black sheep with no acceptance letters, knowing that I would be right there with them if the money and timing were different.

That summer I made the decision to start saving as much money as possible so I could travel in my newfound free time. I became a lifeguard, taught swim lessons, worked at a bakery, and held many yard sales to raise money to get me out of there. However, by the end of summer, some of my mentors and teachers from the Seattle Musical Theater scene had reignited my desire to pursue my education and promised to help me train as hard as possible and get me into college. My parents were also on board with the idea since they felt guilty about things not working out the last time.

While I began my training in the fall, I tried one semester of community college with lackluster results. This put another damper on my spirits about formal education. At the same time, I was auditioning around Seattle to see if I could get any gigs and develop new relationships as a failsafe in case school didn't work out again. I booked my first professional gig and rediscovered my confidence and desire to continue pursuing a Musical Theater education.

By the winter of 2014, I felt more than ready to conquer the Chicago Unified auditions. As an added bonus, I was traveling with my voice teacher and several friends who were also going through the process. My auditions went so well, I was relieved it all happened the way it did, one year later. Had I done this the previous year, I would have been ill prepared, overzealous, and undertrained, not to mention mentally unstable from a crazy senior year at a competitive high school.

I ended up getting into the school of my dreams. However, a family emergency requiring my brother to need extensive medical care and treatment threatened to prevent me from going to college once again. My parents couldn't afford both my college and his treatment, and the money I saved for traveling would not cover a full semester's worth of tuition and the dorms. I was again resigned to stay home and become a theater vagabond. But out of nowhere a close family friend offered to cover the cost of my brother's treatment. I think we were all in shock, because not only was my brother able to get the help he needed, but I was able to begin my career in the arts! Taking a gap year was unexpected but, ultimately, the best decision for me.

Chapter Takeaway

Lemons and Lemonade

We all consider this the worst-case scenario, but as you've seen from just a few student examples, it's not the end of the world. Once you've processed the emotions, it's time to start working on a strong plan B that is a good fit for you. Here are a few concise tips to come back to when you're ready to move forward.

- Before the decisions are made, have a plan about how you will receive your decisions from phone calls, to wait-list notifications, to rejection letters.
- Let your team know what you will need from them during this time, even if it is space alone to process everything.
- If you are put on the Alt/WL, then communicate regularly with that school and make sure they know your interest.
- Be prepared to deposit immediately (if possible).
- In the end, if you aren't accepted to any program you would attend, decide how you want to spend the upcoming year:
  - Attend the university of your top-choice program with the plan to re-audition.
  - Apply to community college or a local university.
  - Consider taking a gap year to refine your skills and reexamine your school list.
  - Hire a coach.
  - Audition for musicals and plays in your home city.
  - Travel.

Remember, there is no one "right way" to study and train in Musical Theater after high school. If you really see yourself in a college program, keep working and improving your skills. A year of focus and drive can make all the difference.

Afterword

"I CHOSE RIGHT"

I want to end this book with the story of a recent graduate named Byron Freeman. Everything that could go wrong in his college audition for Pace Musical Theater did go wrong, but Byron had the resilience, focus, faith, and confidence to handle it and he came out on top. Byron didn't have years of formal Musical Theater training, and he didn't go to a fancy camp or work with a coach. He used the tools that he had access to: doing the research into what schools would be the right fit, choosing material that would be appropriate for him, and, above all, using the adversity of the day to ignite him.

I remember his audition like it was yesterday. He did not let on that anything out of the ordinary happened before he walked in the room; he entered with joy and ownership. The material he chose to sing told me so much about him. He understood who he was and what he was able to bring to the audition and the program as a performer and a person. He showed passion and potential, and he put all of himself into the lyrics of the song. He was physically and emotionally connected and I would never have known what happened prior had he not told me. It is not our policy to accept students on the spot, but every once in a while, when there is someone we feel we must have, we do it!

Here is his audition story:

At my performing arts high school, I was strictly a vocal music major. When I decided to go to college for Musical Theater, not classical music or opera, the voice faculty completely gave up on me. Everyone made me feel like I wasn't talented enough to enter a field with singing, dancing, and acting. To them, I was only a vocalist, nothing else. I was so disappointed that no one was interested in guiding me or helping me be successful, no matter my choice.

So, I began the journey of auditioning for Musical Theater programs all by myself.

I am the ONLY person in my family involved in the performing arts, so when I say all alone, I truly mean it. I had support from my family, but they knew as much as I did about the field, which was close to nothing. I sought out every program in the country for the place that was right for me. I remember doubting myself when I let the perceptions of my teachers get to me, but I knew I had a duty to myself and to anyone else who has been told no, to go full throttle and attack those auditions head-on. I never had a proper acting class in my life, and at the time, I had not been in a proper dance class in about four years. But, instead of letting that hinder me, I turned it into my fuel. I would leave English class every Tuesday and Thursday to take tap with the middle school students, and I read every monologue and play through and through. Then I was ready for my auditions.

I strategically only applied to five schools because I knew the odds of getting in would be easier to handle. Fast forward, I attended every audition and they all went amazing. Finally, there was one audition left on my list, Pace University. Pace was the only school I applied to in New York City because it was my top choice. I saved it for last for good luck, hoping that I would be more comfortable with auditioning by the time I went in. Well. . . things did not go exactly as planned.

Two days before my audition at Pace, I twisted my knee out of the socket during rehearsal for a show. The morning of the audition, I woke up thirty minutes late, which completely threw me. Instantly, I was stressed out. For every other audition, I was super early, dressed to my best, and feeling very healthy, but of course not on the day that mattered most. I ended up throwing on the quickest thing I could iron and even wore bright blue sneakers, which to me was a huge NO, but I truly had no other choice. As if things could not get worse, I was stuck in traffic for thirty minutes. By then, I felt completely defeated.

When I arrived at Pace I was almost an hour late. They told me I was originally in the group to dance first, but since I was so late, they had no other choice but to make me join the singing group. Even though my knee was busted, I was banking on dancing first, because I knew I could have time to relax before having to sing. But it was go time.

I remember sitting upstairs listening to the other people talk about their shows and experiences, and feeling so out of place, especially due to my circumstances that day. So I knew that I needed to go and get quiet with myself. I prayed and simply asked God for my and His best during that time. It was in that moment I remembered the songs that I chose to sing: "Make Them Hear You" from Ragtime *and "Mister's Song" from* The Color Purple. *I chose "Mister's Song" because we were doing the musical at my high school and I was blatantly told that I didn't get the part because my acting just was not good enough, and the role went to a junior. I wanted the chance to prove that I could do the role. Next, I chose "Make Them Hear You" because it resonates with everything I wanted to say for myself and for anyone who has ever been told that they are not good enough.*

So I took all of that into the room and did not care that I was late, injured, or anything. It was my moment to seize opportunity and not succumb to the fate that everyone at my high school thought was written for me. After I sang, I remember Amy Rogers asking me verbatim, "Do you want to go here?" I responded like anyone would and was super excited. Then she came over to me and said, "I don't think you understand, when you go downstairs to dance, I just want you to go and have fun, and not worry about that," pointing to my knee. This sounded like a completely normal conversation, but she went on, "I want you to know that I want you in this program! I am accepting you right here! Today!"

It was shortly after that when I started to cry hysterically and hyperventilate. I could not believe what just happened to me and I was more confused than excited. I had come in thinking that it was going to be one of the worst days of my life, and even with the prayers I made, I had no expectation that something like that would happen at all. But it did, and life for me completely changed. There was a fire in me that had been gone for a while, and a sense of faith that was restored.

I remember going back home in the same car that made me late, with a totally different mindset. In a way, I thank my high school teachers, because it was their lack of support that catapulted me into a world that I never thought possible for me, coming from a place like I do. A young black boy who grew up in the hood going to COLLEGE in New York City to pursue his dreams of becoming an actor is very rare, almost unheard of. On that day, February 22, 2014, my life changed forever, and it is a day I will never forget.

Byron Freeman

Appendix A | Musical Terms

H ERE IS A HANDY GUIDE to common musical terms you will come across when figuring out your audition cuts. It never hurts to look like a smart musician in the audition room, and if you know how to talk about your music, the accompanist will feel more confident about what they are playing. Clear communication will help everyone be on the same page: the first step in achieving a great audition.

- **Ad lib (aka colla voce, rubato, freely):** An indication to an accompanist that he or she should take the tempos and rhythms from the singer. An "ad lib verse" is common at the beginning of standards and Golden Age tunes. For example, in "Someone to Watch over Me," I follow the singer during the "There's a saying old, says that love is blind" part at the beginning, pushing and pulling. The steady tempo kicks in at "There's a somebody I'm longing to see . . ."
- **Arpeggio:** A chord spread where the sounding of notes is played in rapid succession instead of simultaneously.
- **Caesura (or cesura, or "train tracks"):** A break or pause, marked by a double diagonal line.
- **Cut time:** When switching from common time (4/4), cut time means you'll be playing twice as fast. Also referred to as "playing in 2."
- **Downbeat:** The first beat of a bar.
- **Dynamics:** The gradations of volume in music (e.g., forte, piano, crescendo, etc.).
- **Fermata:** A pause (a dot under an arc indicating that you hold that note or rest until you're ready to move on).
- **Half time feel:** A groove that *feels* half as fast—the tempo doesn't technically change, but frequently the note values get doubled (quarter notes become half notes), giving it a more laid-back or heavier quality. "I'm a Part of That" from *The Last Five Years* includes a great example: it goes from the bouncy "chunk-chunk-chunk-chunk" of "One day we're just like 'Leave It to Beaver' " to a half time feel at the chorus ("And then he'll smile, his eyes light up . . .").
- **Ledger lines:** Short lines added below or above the stave to accommodate notes too high or too low for the stave itself.

- **Meter:** The specific rhythm determined by the number of beats and the time value assigned to each note in a measure. The meter determines the pulse or "beat" of the music. If something goes from 3/4 to 6/8, you can refer to it that as a "change in meter."
- **Pickup (or upbeat):** An unaccented beat or beats that occur(s) before the first beat of a measure.
- **Ritard/rit. (note the correct spelling, please!):** The act of holding back/gradually diminishing the speed.
- **Tempo:** The speed or pace of your song (how fast or slow?).
- **Vamp:** One or more bars of music repeated indefinitely as an accompaniment.

Appendix B | Headshots and Résumés

Headshots

You don't need to spend a lot of money on headshots for your college auditions. In fact, you don't need to spend any if you can find someone who takes good photographs to help you. However, they do need to look professional and clean. And, most importantly, they need to look exactly like you. For the most part, your college audition headshot will take you through senior year of college, when you will be ready for your "real world" headshots for showcase and beyond. Therefore, if you were to spend some money here, it would not go to waste—but, again, you don't have to.

If you are getting headshots done by someone who does not specialize in this type of photo, then make sure you do your research so you know what is "standard" for professional headshots. I have included a few examples here, but there are so many more out there. One good resource is the senior showcase website from the different schools you are interested in. Look through the headshots and find ones you like in order to give your photographer examples of how you want yours to look. You can also go to Broadway show websites and see what kinds of headshots those actors have too. I personally like it if your headshot has a border and I prefer that your name is on it. It does not matter if your shot is horizontal or vertical.

Have the photos taken in good light. Natural sunlight or in a well-lit studio is best. They can be framed from your collarbone up and make sure you are showing us your natural personality. You don't need to have a "serious" headshot to be a "serious" actor. The photo should feel open and welcoming and a smile never hurts.

For these auditions, it is recommended that you get about twenty to thirty headshots printed, as you can never know just how many each program will need. Of course, this depends on how many auditions you are planning to do, but assume each school will need two. The headshots should be about $1.00–$2.00 per print. Don't pay more than that.

Your headshot should be printed as an 8-by-10, and your résumé should be taped or stapled to the back. Remember that a normal sheet of paper is 8½-by-11, so you will need to cut your résumé to match the size of your headshot. Make sure you format your resume accordingly.

Question: What If I Cut or Dye My Hair after the Shots?

Answer: A cut of a few inches should not warrant a new shot. But if you are going from long hair to short or drastically changing the color, then maybe you'll need a new pic. Don't forget we see thousands of headshots per audition season and it is the most tangible thing we have to remember you. If it does not look exactly like you or have your name on it, there is a chance that you will get lost in the shuffle or forgotten.

Question: What Should I Wear in My Headshots?

Answer: Solid colors, layers, and tops with great collars work well. Make sure your top is ironed or steamed and lies on your body nicely. Be wary of shirts with too many patterns or stripes and are just too busy. I personally don't like turtlenecks, but that's just me!

Takeaways

Headshot requirements:

- Color photograph
- A white border
- Your name printed on the front of the photo
- 8-by-10 size
- Needs to look EXACTLY like you

Things that do not work as well for headshots:

- A school or graduation photo
- A photo with hair in your face
- A photo that is taken "over the shoulder"
- An "action shot" or dance photo
- A shot in costume or from a show (trust me, it happens)
- High-gloss prints

Résumés

We do not expect you to have an extensive résumé at this point, so don't worry if there is not a ton to fill up the page. We are looking to see what shows you have done so far and how you have trained. We don't need every competition you ever won, or anything from before sixth grade.

Résumé requirements:

- One page only.
- List your name as you want to be referred to, especially if it is different than your given name.
- Your email. If you don't have a "professional" email, now is the time to get one. For example, elphaba4lyfe@la.com will not fly. A good rule is to have your email be some form of your name.

PHOTO B1 Leana's headshots were free because she and her friend took photos of each other for their college auditions.

PHOTO B2 Daniel's headshots were taken by a friend for free. They are good examples of what to wear and also how to frame the shot.

PHOTO B3 Deanna's headshots were free because she was asked to be a senior portrait model her sophomore year of high school. They worked because they still looked like her.

PHOTO B4 Tatiana's headshots closely follow the guidelines—in color, a white border, her name on the photo, and they look exactly like her—with the bonus of still being free from a friend. You really can ask someone you know to take a great picture of you and then print your headshots in this format.

- Your cell phone number. Yes, YOUR number. Not your parent's number, your number.
- The font and style needs to be clean and easy to read with the columns aligned (see the sample résumé if this is confusing).
- Spell check and read for typos. You would not believe how many times I see my own name on a résumé of someone auditioning for me with my name MISSPELLED.
- List your height.
- Include special skills such as instruments you play, languages you speak, gymnastics, etc.
- DO NOT include any dates anywhere.
- DO NOT list your birthday or address.
- DO NOT list your weight.
- If it is important to you to acknowledge which pronoun you wish to go by, you can note that on the résumé.

There is a standard résumé format. Use the one here as a template:

JOHN SMITH

e-mail
(xxx) xxx-xxxx
height

Performance Experience

Ex/ Show Title	Role	Theater
Angels in America	Mr. Lies/Man in Park	Broadway High School
American Idiot	Male Swing	Broadway High School
Next to Normal	Henry	Milburn Stone Theatre
Ragtime	Ensemble	Broadway High School
Hairspray	Ensemble	Broadway Theatre

Awards

2018 - Jimmy Awards - Finalist
2018 - NATS - Musical Theater Finalist
2018 - High School award for Best Actor in a Musical

Training

Subject: Instructor(s)
Camp: French Woods Summer Camp – 6 Years
Acting: Storybook Theater, French Woods
Voice: Elaine Case – Classical and Musical Theater – 6 years.
Ballet: 3 Years
Tap: 1 Year
Jazz: 4 Years

Skills

Classical Violin – 6 years • Gymnastics – 4 years (back tuck/handspring) • Can read music. Fluent in Spanish. • Daphne Rubin-Vega Impersonation • Licensed Driver

INDEX

CPSIA information can be obtained
at www.ICGtesting.com
Printed in the USA
BVHW041159210720
584060BV00003B/6